FEED THE MAN

MEAT

MANTASTIC BBQ RECIPES · **70**

Oscar *Smith*

Smith
Street
Books

Contents

INTRO

Since the dawn of man, we've been putting hunks of meat over the fire and salivating with anticipation while the roasty, meaty cooking smells draw a hungry crowd. We may have refined the process a little over the last 2.5 million years, but the fact is that searing a steak or a burger over a flame-licked grill is still one of the most satisfying ways to cook, especially for friends.

This book is your guide to getting the absolute best out of your grill – whether it's a modest charcoal bucket or a gas-burning beast with all of the bells and whistles – we've got the ultimate recipes for the manliest of gatherings.

Equipment

Some of the essential – and not-so essential (but nice to have) – bits & pieces for getting the most out of your grill.

LONG-HANDLED METAL TONGS

Your most important tool. Any metal tongs will do, but it's best to avoid light-weight aluminium ones as they will bend out of shape and tend to heat up more easily.

GRILL BRUSH

For cleaning. You want a brush with stiff metal bristles. If you have a hotplate (griddle) look for a brush that has a scraper attached to it as well.

METAL SPATULA

Essential for turning burgers and delicate fish.

MEAT THERMOMETER

The secret to perfectly-cooked meat. There are plenty of different types available at prices to suit any budget, but for grilling, I'd definitely recommend a digital thermometer as they give you an instant read.

BASTING BRUSH

For adding all-important flavour during cooking. Brushes with silicone bristles are much easier to clean than the traditional-style ones, and a long handle is preferable to keep your hands from the heat.

METAL SKEWERS

They're reusable, they don't burn and they don't require soaking. Stainless steel is best, and ensure the skewer is slightly oval or square, as it grips the food better. Just remember that they do get hot!

PIZZA STONE

Once you make pizza in your grill, you'll never go back. A pizza stone works especially well in a kettle-shaped cooker as the domed top reflects the heat perfectly.

FISH BASKET

Two wire frames connected by a hinge on one side that can be closed over food and then turned and moved easily using the handles. Brilliant for cooking whole fish.

SMOKER BOX

A great way to get that smoky-flavoured goodness even when cooking with gas. A simple cast-iron or stainless-steel box that you fill with soaked woodchips and place on top of the grill. (It's also simple to create a smoke box using foil.)

Choosing the right grill

There are two main camps when it comes to outdoor grilling: gas or charcoal. Both have their benefits and drawbacks, so it's important to know which will best suit your requirements.

CHARCOAL

There is just no substitute for the distinctive smoky flavour you get from cooking on charcoal. Charcoal grills can also reach higher temperatures than gas grills, allowing for direct, searing heat for perfectly-charred steaks that stay rare in the middle. That said, charcoal is messy to handle, it requires much more forethought and lighting time (you'll need to light your charcoal 30–45 minutes beforehand) and charcoal is more expensive and less commonly-available than gas canisters (especially if you're using good-quality hardwood charcoal). But if convenience is not your main priority, then charcoal grilling is an extremely rewarding way to go.

GAS

Quick, clean and easy, the convenience of a gas grill is hard to beat. A gas grill lights instantly with no other materials required (as long as your gas bottle is full) and usually only takes about 10 minutes to heat. Gas grills also hold their temperatures more steadily and are easy to clean. Some say cooking on gas is a less 'authentic' experience, but if you appreciate the ease of getting home from work, lighting up your grill and having dinner cooked in 15 minutes with no fuss, then a gas grill is a fantastic option.

SIZE

It's important to consider your requirements and available space when buying a grill. There's no sense buying an eight-burner behemoth if you've only got a small balcony to put it on, whereas if you're likely to be regularly cooking for crowds (and have the space) you probably want to consider something on the larger scale.

HOOD

It's absolutely worthwhile getting a grill with a hood or lid. It makes for a much more versatile piece of equipment, allowing you to cook low and slow, roast vegetables or larger pieces of meat, and even hot-smoke fish or ribs.

DURABILITY

This doesn't (always) mean you have to spend a fortune, but, especially if your grill is not going to live undercover, make sure it's made from durable materials. Get yourself a cover if the grill is likely to get wet when it rains.

If you're willing to pay for them, there's a cornucopia of additional features and add-ons available to the outdoor cook. Some are gimmicks, but a few legitimately useful extras you might look out for are:

- **A rotisserie**: wonderful for slow, even cooking, especially whole chickens or a boneless leg of lamb.

- **Warming racks**: useful if you're cooking for a crowd or if you're grilling a variety of meats or vegetables with different cooking times.

- **A light**: speaks for itself, really. Who hasn't had to pull out their phone torch to check if the sausages are done?

- **An internal thermometer**: great if you're planning on roasting or cooking at low temperatures.

- **A wok burner**: definitely something to consider if you don't have a gas stovetop in your kitchen.

Looking after your grill

TIPS FOR CLEANING

Clean your grill after every use: grills are much easier to clean when warm, so, once you're done eating, turn the heat back on for a few minutes. Turn the burners off and give the hotplate and grill a good scrape with a metal brush to dislodge any food or grease. If there's an excess of grease, use paper towel or newspaper to soak it up.

Avoid harsh chemicals: your food is going on there! Edible acids like lemon juice and vinegar are great for cutting grease. Fill a spray bottle with a 1:1 mixture of water and white vinegar and keep it handy for cleaning.

MAINTENANCE

Do a deep-clean: every few months, take the grates and/or hotplate (griddle) out, soak in hot soapy water and give everything a good scrub.

Routinely check for gas leaks: with the gas turned on, run a little soapy water along the gas line and connections. If the water bubbles, there's a leak, and you need to either tighten the connection or replace the line.

Keep it covered: it's well worth getting a cover, especially if your grill is exposed to the elements.

How to tell when your meat is cooked

The best way to ensure perfectly-cooked meat every time is to use a meat thermometer. If you're resting meat before serving (which is definitely recommended), remember that the internal temperature will rise during that time, so remove the meat from the heat a little bit before it reaches your desired temperature.

CHICKEN

Chicken needs to be completely cooked through and never eaten rare. Chicken is cooked when the internal temperature reaches 75°C (165°F). When cooking a whole bird, a meat thermometer should be inserted into the thickest part of the thigh. If you don't have a meat thermometer, pierce the same part of the thigh with a sharp knife – if the juices run clear then the chicken is cooked. If they're pink or red then the chicken needs to be cooked a little longer.

PORK

For many years, pork had to be overcooked to be deemed safe for consumption, but stricter health regulations over the past few decades means pork can now be enjoyed at its best: medium, still with a little blush of pink in the middle. Pork is medium when the internal temperature is at 71°C (160°F).

LAMB

Lamb can be eaten rare, especially lean cuts like backstrap or tenderloin, but is generally at its best somewhere between medium-rare and medium (45–55°C/ 115–130°F).

BEEF

As beef is perfectly delicious eaten raw, ideal internal temperature is entirely up to personal preference (and your desired outcome). For best results you shouldn't go much above 60°C (140°F) as the meat will start to dry out.

Cooking chart

	°C	°F
CHICKEN		
COOKED	75	165
PORK		
MEDIUM	71	160
WELL-DONE	77	170
LAMB		
RARE	35	95
MEDIUM-RARE	45	115
MEDIUM	55	130
MEDIUM-WELL	65	150
WELL-DONE	75	170
BEEF		
RARE	35	95
MEDIUM-RARE	45	115
MEDIUM	55	130
MEDIUM-WELL	65	150
WELL-DONE	75	170

FEED THE MAN
CHICKEN

Menu

CHICKEN

Undoubtedly chicken is the perfect canvas for almost any set of flavours. I'm not sure it ever met a marinade it didn't get along with – from the most simple (a squeeze of lemon, a touch of garlic) to punch-you-in-the-face levels of chilli, herbs and spices.

Every cut of chicken works on a grill. You can even cook a whole bird if your grill has a hood (and let it be said that whoever first thought to pop a can of beer up a chicken's rear-end deserves a medal – check out the recipe on page 24).

The secret to perfect chicken on the grill is to start with a high heat, to caramelise the outside and get those nice smoky charred bits, and then reduce the heat a little for slower cooking to make sure everything's cooked through.

Barbecued
PERI PERI CHICKEN

1.4 kg (3 lb 1 oz) whole chicken,
    butterflied, skin patted dry with
    paper towel
crusty bread, to serve
Portuguese salad (page 136),
    to serve (optional)

Peri peri sauce
5 fresh long red chillies
5 garlic cloves, unpeeled
1 teaspoon dried oregano
1 teaspoon sweet paprika
1 teaspoon soft brown sugar
80 ml (2½ fl oz/⅓ cup) olive oil
50 ml (1¾ fl oz) cider vinegar
1½ teaspoons salt

To make the sauce, first preheat the oven to 220°C (430°F). Place the chillies on a baking tray and roast for 10 minutes. Set aside to cool then roughly chop. Meanwhile, blanch the garlic cloves in boiling water for 30 seconds, then peel and roughly chop. Combine with the chilli and the remaining ingredients in a small saucepan over medium heat and simmer for 2–3 minutes. Allow the mixture to cool, then puree in a blender.

Place the chicken on a tray and coat with the peri peri sauce, reserving some sauce for basting. Cover with plastic wrap and refrigerate for at least 1 hour.

Preheat a hooded barbecue grill to medium and lightly grease with oil.

Place the chicken skin-side down on the grill and cook, covered, for 7–8 minutes. Turn and cook the other side, basting. Continue to cook with the hood closed, turning and basting occasionally, for a further 30 minutes until cooked through.

Serve with crusty bread and, if you like, a side of Portuguese salad.

BRAZILIAN CACHAÇA
CHICKEN SKEWERS

1 kg (2 lb 3 oz) skinless chicken thigh fillets, each cut into 3 pieces
bamboo skewers, soaked in cold water
baby cos (romaine) lettuce leaves, to serve
½ cup coriander (cilantro) leaves
¼ cup mint leaves
1 lime, cut in half

Cachaça marinade
2 tablespoons olive oil
60 ml (2 fl oz/¼ cup) cachaça (see note)
juice of 1 lime
zest of 2 limes
2 garlic cloves, crushed
1 cup mint leaves, torn
1 long red chilli, finely chopped
½ teaspoon paprika
1 teaspoon soft brown sugar
1 teaspoon sea salt flakes

To make the marinade, combine the ingredients in a mixing bowl.

Add the chicken pieces to the marinade, stirring well to coat. Cover the bowl in plastic wrap (or transfer the whole lot to a zip-lock bag) and refrigerate for at least 4 hours or overnight.

Preheat a barbecue grill to medium and lightly grease with oil.

Thread the chicken pieces onto the skewers and cook on the grill, turning occasionally, for about 6–8 minutes until cooked through.

Pile the lettuce leaves onto a serving platter and place the skewers on top. Scatter with the coriander and mint leaves, and squeeze the lime juice over the top.

Note: Cachaça is a popular Brazilian distilled spirit made from sugarcane juice. Locally it may be referred to as 'holy water', 'heart opener' and 'tiger breath'. It is available at large liquor outlets. This recipe is best started a day ahead to allow the sensational bold flavours to develop.

GRILLED BUTTERMILK

CHICKEN

500 ml (17 fl oz/2 cups) buttermilk
4 garlic cloves, crushed
2 teaspoons wholegrain mustard
2 teaspoons hot paprika
3 teaspoons sea salt flakes
1 teaspoon freshly ground black
  pepper
2 sprigs rosemary, leaves roughly
  chopped
1.4 kg (3 lb 1 oz) whole chicken,
  cut into quarters
lemon halves, to serve
green salad and Barbecued potato
  wedges with lime yoghurt
  (page 130), to serve (optional)

Combine the buttermilk, garlic, mustard, paprika, salt, pepper and rosemary in a mixing bowl.

Place the chicken in a large zip-lock bag and pour in the buttermilk mixture. Ensure the chicken pieces are well coated. Refrigerate for at least 8 hours or overnight, turning the bag occasionally to disperse the marinade.

Preheat a hooded barbecue grill to medium and lightly grease with oil.

Remove the chicken from the marinade and drain. Place the chicken onto the grill skin-side down, cover and cook for 20 minutes, turning once after 10 minutes. Turn again and cook for another 5–10 minutes until the chicken is cooked through.

Serve with lemons halves and, if desired, a green salad and Barbecued potato wedges.

Barbecued
CHICKEN BURGERS
WITH BASIL AIOLI

→→ SERVES 4 ←←

4 round wholemeal (whole-wheat)
 buns, split
1 avocado, mashed
1 cup rocket (arugula) leaves
1 large tomato, sliced

Chicken burgers
500 g (1 lb 2 oz) minced (ground)
 chicken
1 garlic clove, finely chopped
¼ cup basil leaves, torn
½ cup flat-leaf (Italian) parsley
 leaves, finely chopped
1 teaspoon dried chilli flakes
1 teaspoon sea salt flakes
½ teaspoon freshly ground black
 pepper
zest and juice of 1 lemon
2 tablespoons dry breadcrumbs
1 egg, lightly beaten

Basil aioli
2 egg yolks, at room temperature
2 garlic cloves, finely chopped
½ teaspoon sea salt flakes
2 tablespoons lemon juice
½ cup basil leaves, roughly
 chopped
185 ml (6 fl oz/¾ cup) mild-
 flavoured olive oil

To make the burgers, combine the ingredients in a large mixing bowl. Mix well using your hands until you can see the herbs are evenly dispersed. Using wet hands, shape the mixture into patties slightly larger than the round of the buns. Place the patties on a plate lined with baking paper and cover with plastic wrap. Refrigerate for 1 hour.

To make the aioli, place the egg yolks, garlic, salt, lemon juice and basil in a food processor and pulse until well combined and creamy. With the motor running, add the oil in a thin, steady stream and keep processing until the mixture thickens. Taste and adjust the seasoning. Refrigerate until needed.

Preheat a barbecue hotplate (griddle) to medium and lightly grease with oil.

Cook the burgers for about 4–5 minutes on each side or until cooked through. Place the buns, cut-side down, on the hotplate to lightly toast. Allow the buns to cool slightly before spreading avocado on the base of each bun, then top with rocket, a chicken burger and a slice of tomato. Dollop the aioli generously on the tomato then top with the remaining bun halves.

Note: The basil aioli recipe makes about 250 ml (8½ fl oz/1 cup). Any remaining aioli can be used on burgers or as a dip for wedges or crudites. It will keep in an airtight container in the fridge for up to 1 week.

TENNESSEE
BEER CAN CHICKEN

-»- **SERVES 4** -«-

1.4 kg (3 lb 1 oz) whole chicken
1 tablespoon olive oil
375 ml (12½ fl oz/1½ cups) can lager-style wheat beer
Barbecued potato wedges with lime yoghurt (page 130), to serve (optional)

Spice rub
2 teaspoons sweet paprika
2 teaspoons smoked paprika
2 teaspoons soft brown sugar
1 teaspoon ground cumin
½ teaspoon ground coriander
½ teaspoon garlic powder
1 teaspoon sea salt flakes

Preheat a hooded barbecue grill to medium–low and lightly grease with oil.

To make the spice rub, mix the ingredients together in a small bowl.

Coat the chicken in olive oil, and season well with the spice rub mix.

Open the beer can and pour out about a third of the beer. Place the cavity of the chicken over the can, legs down, so that the chicken sits upright. Place carefully on the grill, close the lid and cook for about 1½ hours, until the chicken is cooked through. The chicken is done when a meat thermometer placed into the thickest part of the thigh reads 75°C (165°F) at minimum, or the juices run clear when pierced with a skewer.

Remove the chicken carefully from the grill and set aside to rest for 20 minutes before removing the can and carving. For a great match, serve with Barbecued potato wedges.

Apple Cider
CHICKEN DRUMSTICKS

8 chicken drumsticks
1 long red chili, thinly sliced
½ cup mint leaves

Apple cider marinade
250 ml (8½ fl oz/1 cup) apple cider
2 tablespoon peanut oil
2 tablespoons light soy sauce
2 garlic cloves, crushed
2 cm (¾ in) piece ginger, grated
1 fresh red chilli, chopped finely
zest of 1 lemon
¼ teaspoon white pepper

To make the marinade, combine the ingredients in a medium-sized bowl.

Place the drumsticks in a large zip-lock bag. Pour in the marinade and seal, pressing out any excess air. Massage to ensure the chicken is well coated with the marinade, and refrigerate for 4 hours, turning occasionally to evenly distribute the marinade.

Remove the chicken from the refrigerator 30 minutes before cooking to allow to come to room temperature.

Preheat a barbecue grill to medium and lightly grease with oil.

Place the chicken on the grill, cover and cook, turning regularly, for 15 minutes or until cooked through and juices run clear when the meatiest part of the drumstick is pierced with a skewer.

Serve on a platter garnished with the sliced chilli and mint leaves.

Fiery Lemongrass
CHICKEN WINGS

1 kg (2 lb 3 oz) chicken wings
¼ cup coriander (cilantro) leaves
1 bird's eye chilli, finely sliced

Marinade
2 lemongrass stalks, white part
  only, finely chopped
2 bird's eye chillies, finely sliced
4 coriander (cilantro) roots
  and stems, washed and finely
  chopped
4 garlic cloves, finely chopped
2 tablespoons soft brown sugar
1 teaspoon ground turmeric
2 tablespoons peanut oil
juice of 2 limes
2 tablespoons soy sauce
60 ml (2 fl oz/¼ cup) fish sauce

To make the marinade, pound the lemongrass, chilli, coriander and garlic to a paste using a mortar and pestle. Add the sugar and turmeric and mix well. Add the peanut oil, lime juice and sauces, and stir to combine.

Transfer the marinade to a dish that will comfortably fit the chicken wings. Add the chicken and coat well. Cover with plastic wrap and refrigerate for at least 2 hours, or overnight.

Preheat a barbecue grill to medium–low and lightly grease with oil.

Place the chicken wings on the grill and cover with the hood. Cook, turning occasionally, for 25–30 minutes until the marinade has caramelised and charred and the chicken is cooked through.

Pile the wings onto a platter and garnish with the coriander leaves and sliced chilli.

BUTTERFLIED CHICKEN
WITH ROSEMARY OIL

→ SERVES 4–6 ←

1.5 kg (3 lb 5 oz) whole chicken, butterflied, skin patted dry with paper towel
2 lemons, halved

Rosemary oil
¼ cup fresh rosemary leaves, finely chopped
zest of 1 lemon
2 garlic cloves, roughly chopped
¼ teaspoon black pepper
¾ teaspoon sea salt flakes
2 tablespoons olive oil

To make the rosemary oil, pound the rosemary, lemon zest, garlic, pepper and salt to a paste using a mortar and pestle. Add the oil and mix well.

Rub the rosemary oil all over the chicken, coating the skin and underside well. Reserve a tablespoon of the oil for basting.

Cover the chicken with plastic wrap and set aside for 30 minutes to bring it to room temperature.

Preheat a hooded barbecue grill to medium–high and lightly grease with oil.

Place the chicken skin-side down on the grill, cover and reduce heat to low. Cook for 20 minutes, baste the underside with a sprig of rosemary or a basting brush, then turn the chicken over and baste the skin side. Cover and cook for a further 20 minutes.

If the skin requires further browning and crisping, baste the skin side again and turn over to cook until browned.

Remove from the heat, cover loosely with foil and rest for 10 minutes before carving. Serve with lemon for squeezing over.

Spicy Satay
CHICKEN SKEWERS

600 g (1 lb 5 oz) chicken thigh
 fillets, cut evenly into 3 cm
 (1¼ in) strips
bamboo skewers, soaked in cold
 water
iceberg lettuce leaves, to serve
cucumber slices, to serve
½ fresh pineapple, cut into chunks

Marinade

2 lemongrass stalks, white part
 only, thinly sliced
2 garlic cloves, roughly chopped
2 teaspoons finely grated palm
 sugar
1 teaspoon ground coriander
1 teaspoon ground cumin
1 teaspoon ground turmeric
1 tablespoon peanut oil

Peanut sauce

200 g (7 oz) raw unsalted peanuts
12 dried red chillies, deseeded
2 lemongrass stalks, white part
 only, finely chopped
3 French shallots, finely chopped
2 garlic cloves, finely chopped
1 tablespoon ground coriander
2 teaspoons finely grated palm
 sugar
60 ml (2 fl oz/¼ cup) peanut oil
1 tablespoon tamarind paste
1 tablespoon kecap manis
125 ml (4 fl oz/½ cup) coconut
 milk

To make the marinade, pound the lemongrass and garlic into a paste using a mortar and pestle. Add the palm sugar, coriander, cumin, turmeric and oil, and mix well.

Transfer the marinade to a bowl, add the chicken and mix well. Cover with plastic wrap and refrigerate for at least 4 hours or overnight.

To make the sauce, first preheat the oven to 180°C (350°F). Spread the peanuts on a baking tray and roast for about 5 minutes until fragrant and lightly golden. Set aside to cool, then finely chop. Meanwhile, soak the chillies in hot water for 15 minutes. Drain and roughly chop. Place the chilli into a food processor along with the lemongrass, shallots, garlic, coriander, sugar and peanut oil and process until a paste forms. Heat a medium-sized saucepan over medium heat and add the chilli paste. Cook, stirring continuously for 5 minutes. Add 500 ml (17 fl oz/2 cups) of water and bring to the boil, then add the tamarind, kecap manis, peanuts and coconut milk. Simmer for 5 minutes over low heat or until thickened.

Preheat a barbecue grill to medium-high and lightly grease with oil.

Thread 3–4 chicken pieces onto each skewer so that the chicken lies fairly flat. Cook on the grill, turning regularly, for 3–4 minutes until slightly charred and cooked through. (Cooking time will be determined by the thickness of the chicken.)

Arrange the lettuce, cucumber, pineapple and skewers onto plates. Serve with a small bowl of sauce for each person.

Chipotle
CHICKEN BURRITOS

→→ SERVES 4 ←←

500 g (1 lb 2 oz) chicken
  tenderloins, trimmed
2 corn cobs
4 burrito tortillas
400 g (14 oz) tinned black beans,
  rinsed and drained
½ iceberg lettuce, shredded
½ cup coriander (cilantro) leaves

Chipotle marinade
1 tablespoon chipotle chillies
  in adobo sauce, chopped
2 tablespoons honey
3 garlic cloves, crushed
2 teaspoons sea salt

Fresh tomato salsa
3 ripe tomatoes, diced
½ red onion, finely diced
1 fresh jalapeño chilli, finely
  chopped
¼ cup coriander (cilantro)
  leaves, chopped
1 avocado, diced
½ teaspoon salt
juice of ½ lime

Chipotle aioli
2 egg yolks, at room temperature
¼ teaspoon sea salt flakes
juice of ½ lemon
1 small garlic clove, crushed
2 tablespoons chipotle chillies
  in adobo sauce, chopped
250 ml (8½ fl oz/1 cup) mild-
  flavoured olive oil

To make the marinade, combine the ingredients in a medium-sized bowl. Add the chicken, and mix to coat well. Cover with plastic wrap and refrigerate for 1 hour.

To make the salsa, combine the tomato, onion, chilli, coriander and avocado in a medium-sized bowl. Add the salt and lime juice and mix well.

To make the aioli, place the egg yolks, salt, lemon juice, garlic and chipotle into a small food processor. Process on low and add the oil in a thin, steady stream until incorporated.

Preheat a barbecue grill to high and lightly grease with oil.

Grill the corn, turning occasionally, for about 8–10 minutes until well blackened all over. Remove and set aside to cool. Remove the kernels from the cobs using a sharp knife.

Reduce the grill heat to medium. Cook the chicken for about 10 minutes or until cooked through, turning every 3 minutes. The honey will make the chicken more likely to burn, so frequent turning is important.

To assemble the burritos, first warm the tortillas for 5–10 seconds on the grill. Top each burrito with chicken, salsa, corn, beans, lettuce and coriander, and then drizzle with the chipotle aioli. (The key to wrapping a burrito is to not overfill, so make sure no more than a third of the tortilla is covered.) Fold in both sides, and then roll the tortilla to contain the filling.

Note: The aioli recipe makes about 375 ml (12½ fl oz/1½ cups). Any remaining aioli can be used on burgers or as a dip for the Barbecued potato wedges on page 130. It will keep in an airtight container in the fridge for up to 1 week.

FEED THE MAN
PORK

Menu

PORK

Cooking up some pork sausages on a grill would normally represent the most basic form of cooking there is. Anyone with a pair of eyes and one functioning hand could do it (and I'm sure anyone without either of those could still make do). But what if you had made those sausages from scratch? You are guaranteed to blow people's minds if you turn up to a barbecue with a pile of homemade sausages (yes, the recipe is on page 42 and it's much easier than you think). Sausages that you made yourself. With your own bare hands. I don't think 'hero' is too strong a word here.

While sausages are a classic barbecue staple, it's certainly not the only way to do pork in your backyard. Lean tenderloin is deliciously juicy seared on a grill, while fattier cuts like belly are perfect slathered in sticky glaze, and a rack of tender, smoky baby back ribs may do as much for your reputation as a homemade sausage.

PORK TENDERLOIN
WITH MAPLE, GINGER & ORANGE GLAZE

→→ **SERVES 4** ←←

zest and juice of 2 oranges
80 ml (2½ fl oz/⅓ cup) apple
    cider vinegar
5 cm (2 in) piece ginger, peeled
    and finely grated
2 teaspoons dijon mustard
1½ teaspoons smoked paprika
1½ teaspoons sea salt flakes
1 tablespoon olive oil
2–3 pork tenderloins (about
    600 g/1 lb 5 oz in total)
125 ml (4 fl oz/½ cup) pure
    maple syrup
Chargrilled witlof (page 135),
    to serve (optional)

In a small saucepan, combine the orange zest and juice, vinegar, ginger, mustard, paprika and salt. Simmer over medium–low heat for 3–4 minutes. Set aside to cool.

Transfer 60 ml (2 fl oz/¼ cup) of the marinade to a large zip-lock bag along with the oil. Add the pork and seal, pushing out as much of the air as you can. Massage the marinade into the pork and place in the refrigerator for at least 1 hour.

Meanwhile, add the maple syrup to the remaining marinade in the saucepan to make the glaze. Simmer for 4–5 minutes until reduced and thickened slightly. Reserve half the glaze for serving.

Preheat a barbecue grill to medium-high and lightly grease with oil.

Cook the pork for 2 minutes each side until browned all over. Reduce the heat to medium–low and cook, turning and basting with the glaze, for a further 10–12 minutes or until cooked through.

Cover the pork and rest for 5 minutes.

Cut the pork into 1 cm (½ in) slices and spoon the reserved glaze over the top. If desired, serve with Chargrilled witlof.

GRILLED PORK RIBS
WITH VIETNAMESE DIPPING SAUCE

1.5 kg (3 lb 5 oz) pork spare or
   baby back rib racks, cut into
   individual ribs
iceberg lettuce leaves, to serve
fresh mint sprigs, to serve
coriander (cilantro) sprigs, to serve
cucumber cut into sticks, to serve
small red chillies, sliced, to serve

Marinade
4 French shallots, sliced
4 spring onions (scallions), roughly
   chopped
1 lemongrass stalk, white part only,
   chopped
1 cup coarsely chopped coriander
   (cilantro) stems, roots and leaves
5 cm (2 in) piece ginger, peeled
   and sliced
6 garlic cloves, peeled
80 ml (2½ fl oz/⅓ cup) fish sauce
2 tablespoons soy sauce
1 tablespoon rice vinegar
2 tablespoons palm sugar
1 teaspoon ground white pepper

Dipping sauce
60 ml (2 fl oz/¼ cup) fish sauce
2 tablespoons rice vinegar
2 tablespoons caster sugar
2 garlic cloves, finely chopped
1 small red chilli, finely sliced
2 tablespoons lime juice

To make the marinade, place the ingredients in a food processor and process until finely chopped.

Place the pork ribs in a large bowl and coat well with the marinade. Cover with plastic wrap and refrigerate for up to 5 hours, tossing occasionally.

Preheat a hooded barbecue grill to medium–low and lightly grease with oil.

Place the ribs bone-side down on the grill, reserving the marinade for basting. Cover and cook, basting with the marinade every 15 minutes, for 1 hour. Turn the ribs, baste and reduce heat to low. Cover and cook for a further 30 minutes until tender.

Meanwhile, to make the dipping sauce, combine the fish sauce, vinegar and sugar with 80 ml (2½ fl oz/⅓ cup) water in a small saucepan over medium heat. Bring to just below boiling point then set aside to cool. Add the garlic, chilli and lime juice, and stir to combine.

Transfer the ribs to a serving platter and arrange the lettuce, mint, coriander, cucumber and chilli around them. Serve the dipping sauce in small individual bowls.

Homemade Pork & Fennel
SAUSAGES

→→ MAKES 1 KG (2 LB 3 OZ) SAUSAGES ←←

2 tablespoons fennel seeds
1 kg (2 lb 3 oz) minced (ground)
   pork, at least 30% fat content
   (see note)
1 tablespoon ground black pepper
1 tablespoon salt
2 teaspoons dried chilli flakes
   (optional)
60 ml (2 fl oz/¼ cup) chilled dry
   white wine
natural sausage casings (see note)

Note: Sausage casings can be ordered through your local butcher. Natural casings are best. Casings are stored salted so must be rinsed inside and out with cold water before use.

Note: You can ask your butcher to mince your choice of cut for sausages – scotch fillet, shoulder and belly pork are all ideal. A fairly coarse grind and a minimum of 30% fat will give you the best result.

Toast the fennel seeds in a small dry frying pan over medium heat until fragrant. Transfer to a large mixing bowl and add the pork, pepper, salt and chilli flakes (if using). Using your hands, mix well until the mixture becomes sticky. (This is an important step as it will improve the final texture.) Add the wine and continue to mix.

The flavouring can be checked at this stage by cooking a spoonful of pork mixture in a small frying pan with a little olive oil over medium–high heat. Taste and adjust the seasoning if necessary.

Run cold tap water through the sausage casing until the water runs clean. Cut a length of casing about 2 metres (2 yards) long and feed the casing onto the nozzle of a sausage maker. Leave a bit of casing hanging over to allow any excess air to escape. Feed the mince through the machine or nozzle, assisting the casing to slide off the nozzle as it is filled. Press out any air bubbles. Tie the end in a knot, and working towards the untied end, twist the filled casing into sausage lengths. Tie the open end in a knot. (If you don't have a sausage maker you can make the sausages by hand using a wide-necked funnel.)

Place the sausages onto a plate and cover with a clean dish towel. Refrigerate overnight or up to 48 hours before cooking (this allows the flavours to develop and also reduces the likelihood of the skins splitting).

Preheat a barbecue grill to medium and lightly grease with oil.

Cook the sausages, turning occasionally for about 10 minutes until cooked through.

Jamaican Jerk
PORK BELLY

1.5 kg (3 lb 5 oz) pork belly
Apple & cabbage slaw (page 134),
 to serve (optional)

Jerk marinade
6 spring onions (scallions), roughly
 chopped
2 garlic cloves, roughly chopped
3 scotch bonnet chillies, deseeded
 (if you prefer less heat) and sliced
2 cm (¾ in) piece ginger, peeled
 and grated
2 tablespoons soft brown sugar
2 tablespoons fresh thyme leaves
2 tablespoons ground allspice
1 tablespoon sea salt flakes
2 teaspoons nutmeg
2 teaspoons ground cinnamon
2 bay leaves, torn
125 ml (4 fl oz/½ cup) olive oil
60 ml (2 fl oz/¼ cup) soy sauce
juice of 1 lime
zest and juice of 1 orange
125 ml (4 fl oz/½ cup) cider
 vinegar

To make the marinade, place the ingredients in a food processor and blend until smooth.

Place the pork in a baking dish. Pour the marinade over and massage into the pork. Cover with plastic wrap and refrigerate for at least 2 hours, or overnight.

Preheat a barbecue grill to medium—high and lightly grease with oil.

Place the pork on the grill, reserving the excess marinade for basting. Cook for 10—15 minutes on each side, then reduce the heat to low. Continue to cook, basting and turning every 20 minutes for 1½ hours, or until dark and tender.

Remove from heat, cover and rest for 15 minutes before slicing.

Delicious eaten with Apple & cabbage slaw.

Southern-style
BABY BACK PORK RIBS

→→ **SERVES 4** ←←

1.5 kg (3 lb 5 oz) pork baby back ribs, cut into racks of 4 ribs each
Grilled cabbage salad (page 150), to serve (optional)

Dry rub
2 tablespoons sea salt flakes
1½ tablespoons sweet paprika
2 teaspoons smoked paprika
2 teaspoons garlic powder
1 teaspoon dried oregano
1 teaspoon celery salt
1 teaspoon chilli flakes

Barbecue sauce
½ red onion, finely chopped
2 garlic cloves, finely chopped
2 tablespoons soft brown sugar
1 teaspoon sweet paprika
½ teaspoon smoked paprika
125 ml (4 fl oz/½ cup) tomato ketchup
60 ml (2 fl oz/¼ cup) cider vinegar
60 ml (2 fl oz/¼ cup) pure maple syrup

Preheat a hooded barbecue grill to low heat.

To make the dry rub, combine the ingredients in a small bowl.

Coat the ribs in the dry rub, then wrap in foil. Place 2–3 racks in each foil package for easy handling.

Place the foil packs onto the grill and cover. Cook for 2 hours, turning every 30 minutes.

Meanwhile, to make the barbecue sauce, combine the ingredients in a small saucepan with 250 ml (8½ fl oz/1 cup) water. Cook over low heat for 20–25 minutes until thick. Reserve half the sauce for serving.

Remove the foil packages from the grill. Increase the heat to medium and lightly grease with oil. Carefully unwrap the ribs and discard the foil. Brush the ribs all over with the remaining barbecue sauce and return to the grill. Cook, basting and turning regularly, for 30 minutes, until the ribs are browned and sticky, caramelised and charred.

Pile the ribs onto a serving platter and serve with the reserved barbecue sauce and, if desired, Grilled cabbage salad.

KOREAN
BARBECUED PORK

→→ **SERVES 6** ←←

1 kg (2 lb 3 oz) pork belly, cut into
   8 cm (3¼ in) pieces, then very
   thinly sliced
oakleaf lettuce leaves, to serve
spring onions (scallions) cut into
   10 cm (4 in) lengths, to serve
sliced green chillies, to serve
toasted sesame seeds, to serve

Marinade
½ onion, sliced
½ cup grated nashi pear
3 spring onions (scallions), finely
   chopped
4 garlic cloves, crushed
½ teaspoon grated ginger
3 tablespoons gochujang (Korean
   red pepper paste)
45 g (1½ oz/¼ cup) soft brown
   sugar
2 tablespoons rice cooking wine
1 tablespoon soy sauce
2 teaspoons sesame oil
1 tablespoon sesame seeds
2 tablespoons fish sauce

To make the marinade, combine the ingredients in a large bowl. Season with pepper. Add the pork and mix to coat well. Cover with plastic wrap and refrigerate for at least 2 hours.

Heat a barbecue hotplate (griddle) to high and lightly grease with oil.

Cook the pork in batches. Place pieces of pork on the hotplate in a single layer (avoid crowding). Cook for 2 minutes on each side or until caramelised. Transfer to a serving plate and keep warm while the remaining pork is cooked.

Arrange the lettuce leaves, spring onions, chillies on the serving plate around the pork. Sprinkle with the sesame seeds and serve.

FEED THE MAN
SEAFOOD

Menu

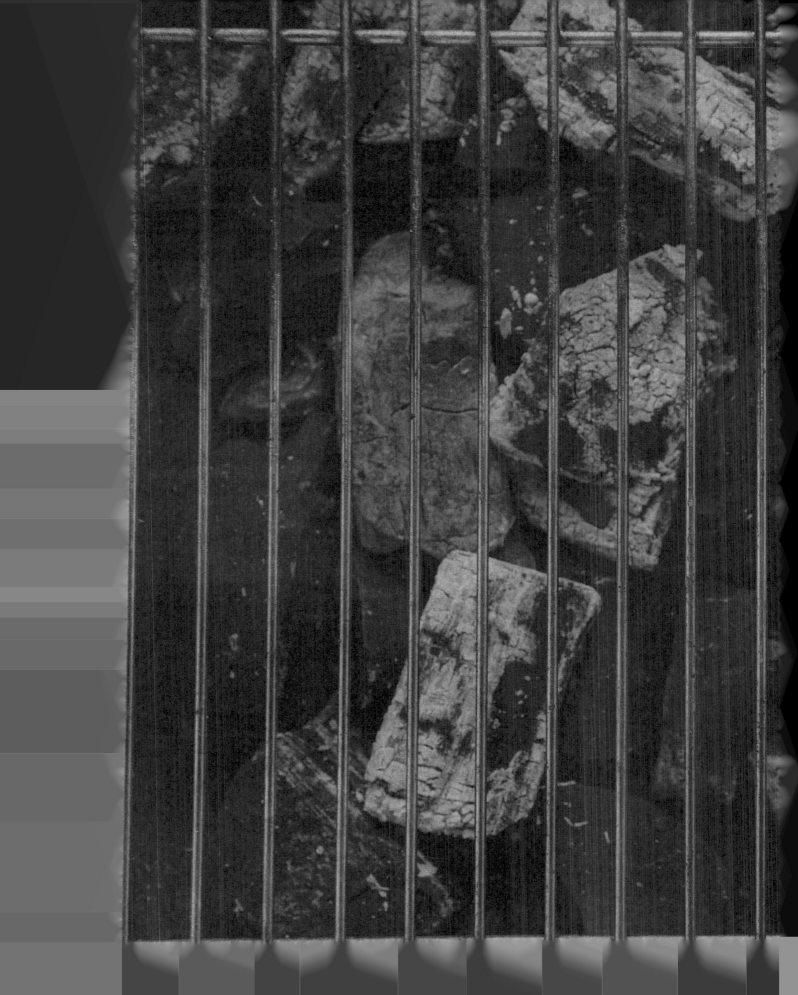

SEAFOOD

While cooking a big hunk of red meat over the fire is undeniably manly, let's be honest, it's manly in a bit of caveman kind of way. The modern, sophisticated man may wish to show his prowess with a little more finesse and subtlety.

A giant T-bone gets the job done, but a whole flounder with burnt butter, capers and sage (page 56)? That gets the job done with class. And sure, everyone loves a grilled chicken satay skewer but wouldn't you rather be the guy serving up grilled lobster tail and salad sliders (page 62)?

Cooking seafood on a grill couldn't be simpler and will lift your game to even greater heights. Just make sure you give your grill a good clean and oil before cooking fish and shellfish as the delicate flesh can stick easily due to the high cooking temperatures.

SPICED FISH TACOS
WITH CHIPOTLE SAUCE

→ SERVES 4–6 ←

1 kg (2 lb 3 oz) firm white fish (such as snapper or ling), cut into 10 cm x 3 cm (4 in x 1¼ in) pieces
olive oil, for brushing
2 cups coriander (cilantro) leaves, roughly chopped
1 white onion, very finely chopped
¼ green cabbage, finely shredded
6 radishes, thinly shaved
12 corn tortillas
3 limes, cut into wedges

Chipotle sauce
125 g (4½ oz/½ cup) whole egg mayonnaise
125 g (4½ oz/½ cup) Greek-style yoghurt
1 small chipotle chilli in adobo sauce, finely chopped, plus 1 teaspoon of sauce
½ teaspoon dried oregano
1 tablespoon finely chopped dill
zest and juice of 1 lime

Spice mix
1 teaspoon paprika
½ teaspoon ground cumin
½ teaspoon freshly ground black pepper
½ teaspoon dried oregano
½ teaspoon sea salt flakes

To make the sauce, place the ingredients in a blender and blend until smooth. Transfer to a serving bowl and season to taste. Cover with plastic wrap and refrigerate until needed.

Preheat a barbecue hotplate (griddle) to medium–high and lightly grease with oil.

To make the spice mix, combine the ingredients in a small bowl.

Pat the fish dry with paper towel, then brush with olive oil and sprinkle with the spice mix. Cover with plastic wrap and refrigerate for 10 minutes.

Combine the coriander and onion in a small bowl.

Cook the fish, turning once, for approximately 2 minutes each side or until just cooked through.

Toast the tortillas on one side on the hotplate or grill for about 30 seconds or until lightly charred.

Serve the fish in a pile on a board or platter along with the tortillas, chipotle sauce, coriander and onion, a pile of the cabbage and radishes, and lime wedges.

Louisiana
PRAWN PO'BOY

→→ SERVES 4 ←←

600 g (1 lb 5 oz) large green
   prawns, shelled and deveined
bamboo skewers, soaked in cold
   water
1 long baguette, cut into 4 lengths
   then halved
2 cucumbers, sliced into thin
   lengths
½ green oakleaf lettuce, washed
   and drained thoroughly

Louisiana marinade
2 tablespoons olive oil
1 garlic clove, finely chopped
1 teaspoon sweet paprika
½ teaspoon salt
¼ teaspoon freshly ground black
   pepper
¼ teaspoon cayenne pepper
½ teaspoon dried oregano
½ teaspoon dried thyme

Remoulade
125 g (4½ oz/½ cup) good-quality
   whole egg mayonnaise
1 teaspoon dijon mustard
juice of ½ lemon
2 teaspoons capers, roughly
   chopped
¼ teaspoon cayenne pepper
¼ teaspoon sweet paprika

To make the marinade, combine the ingredients in a large mixing bowl. Add the prawns and toss to coat well. Cover and refrigerate for 30 minutes.

To make the remoulade, combine the ingredients in a small mixing bowl. Mix well and set aside.

Heat the barbecue grill to medium and lightly grease with oil.

Thread the prawns onto the bamboo skewers and cook for 2–3 minutes on each side.

Fill the baguettes with cucumber and lettuce. Remove the prawns from the skewers and pile onto the lettuce. Top with remoulade and serve.

Whole Flounder
WITH BURNT BUTTER,
CAPERS & SAGE

→→ SERVES 4 ←←

4 x 500 g (1 lb 2 oz) flounder,
  rinsed and dried
2 tablespoons olive oil
banana leaves, for wrapping
100 g (3½ oz) butter
⅓ cup capers, drained
20 sage leaves
lemon cheeks, to serve

Brush each flounder with oil and season with salt.

Place a large sheet of foil onto a clean work surface. Cover with a banana leaf. Place one flounder on the banana leaf, top-side down, and wrap carefully to enclose.

Repeat with the remaining fish.

Preheat a barbecue hotplate (griddle) to medium–high and lightly grease with oil.

Cook the flounder for 4–5 minutes, turn and continue cooking for 2–3 minutes until cooked through.

Meanwhile, place a small frying pan on the hotplate to heat. Add the butter and swirl in the pan to heat evenly. When it starts to foam, add the capers and sage and cook for 1 minute or until crisp.

Serve each flounder on its banana leaf and spoon the hot butter, capers and sage over the top, with a lemon cheek alongside.

Whole Snapper
WITH THAI FLAVOURS

→→ **SERVES 4** ←←

3 long red chillies, deseeded and coarsely chopped

2 lemongrass stalks, white part only, thinly sliced

1 tablespoon grated palm sugar

½ bunch coriander (cilantro), leaves picked and stems roughly chopped

1 tablespoon fish sauce

2 tablespoons coconut milk

1 kg (2 lb 3 oz) whole snapper, cleaned and scaled

2 limes, sliced, plus extra lime wedges to serve

4 kaffir lime leaves, torn

banana leaves, for wrapping

Preheat a barbecue grill to medium-high and lightly grease with oil.

Pound the chillies, lemongrass, palm sugar and coriander to a coarse paste using a mortar and pestle. Transfer to a small mixing bowl, add the fish sauce and coconut milk and stir to combine.

Lay the banana leaves out on a large board, overlapping to form a piece large enough to wrap the fish.

Make four diagonal, 1 cm (½ in) deep cuts in each side of the snapper. Coat the top of the fish with half the chilli paste, working it into the cuts. Place the fish, paste-side down, in the centre of the banana leaves. Fill the cavity with lime slices and kaffir lime leaves and spread the chilli paste over the fish. Wrap the banana leaves to enclose, then wrap in foil.

Place the parcel on the grill and cook for 8 minutes on each side, until just cooked through.

Serve with lime wedges.

GRILLED TUNA
WITH GARLIC & CAPER AIOLI

4 tuna steaks, 2 cm (¾ in) thick
Summer veg ratatouille parcels
  (page 128), to serve (optional)

Garlic & caper aioli
2 garlic cloves, crushed
1 teaspoon sea salt flakes
2 egg yolks
250 ml (8½ fl oz/1 cup) olive oil
1 tablespoon lemon juice
1½ tablespoons baby capers,
  drained
1 tablespoon finely chopped
  flat-leaf (Italian) parsley

Marinade
zest of 1 lemon, finely grated
1 tablespoon sea salt flakes
1 teaspoon coarse ground black
  pepper
60 ml (2 fl oz/¼ cup) olive oil

To make the aioli, place the garlic, salt and egg yolks in a small food processor and blend until well combined. With the motor running, add the oil in a thin, steady stream, until the aioli thickens. Transfer to a small bowl. Stir in the lemon juice, capers and parsley. Cover and refrigerate until required.

To make the marinade, combine the ingredients in a small bowl. Brush the tuna with the marinade and place in a zip-lock bag and refrigerate for at least 2 hours, or overnight.

Preheat a barbecue grill to high and lightly grease with oil.

Allow the tuna to come to room temperature before cooking.

Cook the tuna steaks for about 2 minutes until the red tuna turns beige part of the way up the side. Turn and cook for another 2 minutes, until the colour of the tuna changes as before and you can just see a line of pink from the side.

Serve with a generous dollop of the aioli, and if you like, Summer veg ratatouille parcels to accompany.

JAPANESE
SEVEN-SPICE CALAMARI

→→ **SERVES 4** ←←

500 g (1 lb 2 oz) squid hoods, cleaned and cut into 2 cm (¾ in) rings, leave tentacles intact

2 tablespoons sesame seeds, toasted until golden

2 spring onions (scallions), thinly sliced on the diagonal

Japanese marinade

125 ml (4 fl oz/½ cup) light soy sauce

5 cm (2 in) piece of ginger, peeled and finely grated (approximately 2 tablespoons)

3 tablespoons mirin

1 tablespoon shichimi tōgarashi (see note)

1 tablespoon peanut oil

To make the marinade, combine the ingredients in a large bowl. Reserve half the marinade for basting.

Add the squid to the remaining marinade and mix well to coat. Set aside in the refrigerator to marinate for 15 minutes.

Preheat a barbecue grill to high and lightly grease with oil.

Grill the squid, turning frequently and basting with reserved marinade, for 2–3 minutes until opaque and tender. Take care not to overcook the squid as it can quickly become rubbery.

Serve garnished with toasted sesame seeds and spring onions.

Note: Shichimi tōgarashi is a traditional Japanese seven-spice mix, predominately made up of red pepper, and is available from Asian supermarkets.

Lobster Tail & SALAD SLIDERS

→→ **MAKES 8 SLIDERS** ←←

2 tablespoons butter, softened
2 tablespoons finely chopped
  flat-leaf (Italian) parsley
zest of 1 lemon
pinch of sea salt flakes
2 lobster tails, halved lengthways
1 stick celery, finely sliced
½ red apple, finely sliced
1 tablespoon finely chopped dill
2 tablespoons whole egg
  mayonnaise
2 tablespoons crème fraiche
1 butter lettuce, leaves separated
8 slider buns, split and toasted

Preheat barbecue grill to high and lightly grease with oil.

Combine the butter, parsley, lemon zest and salt in a bowl.

Place the lobster tail halves, cut-side down, on the grill and cook for 2–3 minutes until slightly charred. Turn and spread lobster tails with the seasoned butter. Continue grilling for a further 3–5 minutes until the lobster meat is tender. Remove from the heat, cover loosely and set aside to cool.

Toss the celery, apple and dill together a bowl. Add the mayonnaise and crème fraiche and mix well.

Remove the lobster meat from the shells and chop into 1 cm (½ in) discs. Stir gently into the salad, coating well with the dressing.

Place the lettuce leaves onto the bun bases, and divide the salad equally between the buns. Top with the lids and secure with toothpicks. Serve immediately.

Crispy Skin Salmon
WITH FENNEL
& CELERY REMOULADE

→→ **SERVES 4** ←←

4 x 200 g (7 oz) skin-on salmon
   fillets
lemon cheeks, to serve

**Fennel & celery
remoulade**

3 tablespoons whole egg
   mayonnaise
60 g (2 oz/¼ cup) Greek-style
   yoghurt
1 teaspoon dijon mustard
1 tablespoon finely chopped
   flat-leaf (Italian) parsley
1 tablespoon finely chopped
   chives
2 teaspoons finely chopped
   tarragon
1 tablespoon roughly chopped
   capers
2 cornichons, finely chopped
2 fennel bulbs, halved lengthways,
   cored and shaved
2 celery stalks, thinly sliced
   on the diagonal

To make the remoulade, combine the mayonnaise, yoghurt and mustard in a large mixing bowl. Add the parsley, chives, tarragon, capers and cornichons and stir thoroughly. Mix in the fennel and celery and season with pepper to taste. Cover with plastic wrap and refrigerate until required.

Preheat a barbecue hotplate (griddle) to high and lightly grease with oil.

Pat the salmon skin dry with paper towel and sprinkle generously with salt. Cover and allow to rest for 20 minutes to bring to room temperature. The salt will cause the salmon skin to release moisture so pat dry again and sprinkle with a little more salt before cooking.

Cook the salmon skin-side down for 4 minutes until crisp and golden. Turn the fillets and cook for another 1–2 minutes, depending on the thickness of the fillets, until medium rare.

Serve the salmon with the remoulade and lemon cheeks.

FEED THE MAN

LAMB

Menu

LAMB

There's something special about lamb. It has a particularly distinctive flavour – you could never mistake it for anything else – it pairs so well with bold seasonings and yet, is often at its best with nothing but a liberal sprinkling of salt. And boy, does lamb love salt.

Lamb is generally pretty tender, so even the tougher, more economical cuts like forequarter (shoulder) chops are perfect for the grill. And if you want to splash out a little, a lamb cutlet (rib chop), seared on both sides and served with a squeeze of lemon and a bit of salt is the best damn meat lollipop you'll ever have.

Moroccan
LAMB MEATBALLS
WITH MINTED YOGHURT

➤➤ **SERVES 4–6** ◄◄

Unleavened grilled flatbread
 (page 125), to serve
½ red onion, finely sliced
chopped mint, to serve
chopped flat-leaf (Italian) parsley,
 to serve
halved cherry tomatoes, to serve

Moroccan meatballs
1 tablespoon ground cumin
1 tablespoon sweet paprika
4 garlic cloves, finely chopped
1 teaspoon sea salt flakes
½ cup coriander (cilantro) leaves,
 chopped
juice of ½ lemon
1 egg
2 tablespoons olive oil
2 tablespoons pine nuts, lightly
 toasted and roughly chopped
1 kg (2 lb 3 oz) minced (ground)
 lamb

Minted yoghurt
250 g (9 oz/1 cup) natural yoghurt
pinch of sugar
1 tablespoon finely chopped mint

To prepare the meatballs, combine the cumin, paprika, garlic, salt, coriander, lemon juice, egg, olive oil and pine nuts in a large mixing bowl. Add the lamb and mix well using your hands. Using wet hands, roll the mixture into golf ball-sized balls and flatten slightly into thick patties. Place on a tray, cover with plastic wrap and refrigerate for 1 hour.

Preheat a barbecue hotplate (griddle) to medium and lightly grease with oil.

To make the minted yoghurt, combine the ingredients in a bowl.

Cook the meatballs, turning occasionally, for about 7–8 minutes until cooked through.

Toast the flatbreads on one side only for 20 seconds until warmed through and a little charred in places.

Serve by loading each uncharred side of the flatbread with onion, mint, parsley, tomato, a few meatballs and then drizzling with minted yoghurt.

GRILLED LAMB LOIN
WITH ANCHOVY & GARLIC BUTTER

2 tablespoons olive oil
½ teaspoon sea salt flakes
2 sprigs rosemary, roughly
  chopped
8 thick lamb loin chops

Anchovy & garlic butter
6 anchovies, finely chopped
2 garlic cloves, crushed
2 tablespoons finely chopped
  flat-leaf (Italian) parsley
zest of ½ lemon
125 g (4½ oz) butter, softened

To make the butter, pound the anchovies, garlic, parsley and lemon zest to a paste using a mortar and pestle. Combine with the butter and mix well. Lay a sheet of baking paper on a work surface and spoon the butter into a thick line in the centre. Roll into a log and chill until needed.

In a small bowl, combine the oil, salt and rosemary. Brush the lamb chops with the oil, cover with plastic wrap and set aside for 30 minutes to come to room temperature.

Preheat a barbecue grill to high and lightly grease with oil.

Cook the lamb chops for 3–4 minutes on each side for medium, or 4–5 minutes on each side for well done. Transfer to a plate, cover loosely with foil and rest for 5 minutes.

Slice the anchovy butter into discs and serve on the lamb chops.

Greek-Style Slow-Cooked
LAMB ROAST

→→ **SERVES 6** ←←

4 sprigs rosemary
4 sprigs mint
8 sprigs oregano
1 small bunch thyme
4 sprigs lemon balm
1 lemon, sliced
6 garlic cloves, unpeeled
2.5 kg (5½ lb) lamb leg
2 tablespoons olive oil
1 teaspoon sea salt flakes
½ teaspoon cracked black pepper
green salad and Summer veg
  ratatouille parcels (page 128),
  to serve (optional)

Preheat a hooded barbecue grill to low and lightly grease with oil.

Line a baking tin with baking paper and spread half the herbs, lemon slices and garlic over the bottom.

Rub the lamb leg with olive oil, salt and pepper, and place it on top of the herbs. Put the remaining herbs, lemon and garlic on and around the lamb.

Place the baking tin on the grill, cover and cook for up to 5 hours, until the lamb is caramelised and tender (cooking time will depend on the barbecue heat and the size of the roast). After cooking for 3 hours, check for doneness every 30 minutes, replacing the cover and continuing to cook if required.

Remove from the heat, cover in foil and rest for 20 minutes before carving.

This roast is great served with a green salad and Summer veg ratatouille parcels.

Spicy Kashmiri
ROAST LAMB

1.5 kg (3 lb 5 oz) butterflied
  boneless lamb leg
125 g (4½ oz/½ cup) natural
  yoghurt
½ cup almonds
1 tablespoon honey

Kashmiri spice mix
2 cm (¾ in) ginger, grated
4 garlic cloves, crushed
1 small red chilli, finely chopped
1½ teaspoons sea salt flakes
1 teaspoon ground cumin
1 teaspoon ground turmeric
½ teaspoon ground cardamom
½ teaspoon freshly ground black
  pepper
juice of ½ lemon
2 tablespoons olive oil

Preheat a hooded barbecue grill to medium and lightly grease with oil.

To make the spice mix, combine the ingredients in a small bowl. Rub all over the lamb to coat well.

Blend the yoghurt, almonds and honey in a food processor until smooth. Coat the spiced lamb with the yoghurt mixture.

Place the lamb on the grill and cook, covered, for about 40 minutes, turning once halfway through. Cooking times will vary; if lamb is still rare, turn again and cook for a further 10–15 minutes or until cooked through. Remove from the heat, cover and rest for 15 minutes before slicing.

RACK OF LAMB
WITH ROSEMARY CRUST

2 racks of lamb, with 6–8 points on each rack

1 tablespoon olive oil, plus extra for brushing

2 garlic cloves, crushed

1 tablespoon wholegrain mustard

zest of 1 lemon

2 sprigs fresh rosemary, finely chopped

2 tablespoons finely chopped flat-leaf (Italian) parsley

1 tablespoon dry breadcrumbs

Cut the lamb racks in half, to make 4 racks of 3–4 cutlets each. Brush the racks with olive oil and season on both sides with salt and pepper.

In a small bowl, combine 1 tablespoon of olive oil with the garlic, mustard and lemon zest. Place lamb racks bone-side down on a tray and spread the mustard mixture evenly onto the fat side.

Combine the rosemary, parsley and breadcrumbs in a small bowl. Press the mixture firmly into the mustard to help it adhere. Set aside to rest for 30 minutes.

Preheat a hooded barbecue grill to medium high heat and lightly grease with oil.

Cook the lamb racks, crust-side down, for 3 minutes, then turn and cook for another 6 minutes. Lower the heat to medium. Stand the racks upright, leaning against each other to balance, then cover the barbecue and cook for 15–20 minutes or until done to your liking.

Remove the lamb from the heat, cover loosely with foil and rest for 10 minutes before slicing into cutlets to serve.

Mint & Garlic
LAMB KEBABS
WITH QUINOA TABOULI

➤➤ **MAKES 10 SKEWERS** ◄◄

1 kg (2 lb 3 oz) boneless lamb leg, cut into 5 cm (2 in) cubes

10 tiny onions (I use pickling onions), peeled and halved

2 zucchini (courgettes), cut into 2 cm (¾ in) rounds

Unleavened or Yeasted grilled flatbread (pages 124–125), to serve (optional)

Roasted chickpea & garlic hommus, (page 139), to serve (optional)

Marinade
250 g (9 oz/1 cup) natural yoghurt

2 tablespoons extra-virgin olive oil

2 garlic cloves, roughly chopped

zest and juice of 1 lemon

½ cup mint leaves

¼ cup flat-leaf (Italian) parsley leaves

3 teaspoons sea salt flakes

1 teaspoon cracked black pepper

Quinoa tabouli
100 g (3½ oz/½ cup) red quinoa, well rinsed

1½ cups flat-leaf (Italian) parsley leaves, finely chopped

1 cup mint leaves, finely sliced

1 tablespoon chopped oregano

4 spring onions (scallions), very finely sliced

3 roma (plum) tomatoes, diced

80 ml (2½ fl oz/⅓ cup) lemon juice

80 ml (2½ fl oz/⅓ cup) extra-virgin olive oil

To make the marinade, blend the yoghurt, olive oil, garlic, lemon zest and juice, mint, parsley, salt and pepper until smooth using a blender or food processor.

Place the lamb in a large zip-lock bag and pour in the marinade. Seal the bag, pushing out as much air as possible. Massage the bag to ensure the lamb is well coated in the marinade. Refrigerate for 4–8 hours.

To make the tabouli, bring a small saucepan of water to boil and cook the quinoa over medium–low heat for 15 minutes or until tender. Drain and set aside to cool. Combine the quinoa, parsley, mint, oregano, spring onions and tomatoes in a large serving bowl. Whisk together the lemon juice and olive oil and season to taste. Pour over the quinoa mixture and toss well.

Preheat a barbecue grill to medium–high and lightly grease with oil.

Thread cubes of marinated lamb onto 10 flat metal skewers, alternating with pieces of onion and zucchini.

Cook the kebabs for about 8–12 minutes, turning, until browned all over and cooked through.

Transfer the kebabs to a platter and rest for 5 minutes. If desired, serve with Grilled flatbread and Roasted chickpea & garlic hommus.

Chermoula
LAMB SHOULDER
WITH GARLIC & TAHINI YOGHURT

1 kg (2 lb 3 oz) butterflied boneless
  lamb shoulder
chopped coriander (cilantro)
  leaves, to serve
chopped flat-leaf (Italian) parsley,
  to serve

Chermoula
2 teaspoon cumin seeds
2 teaspoons coriander seeds
1 small onion, roughly chopped
3 garlic cloves, crushed
2 cm (¾ in) ginger, finely grated
zest and juice of 1 lemon
1 cup coriander (cilantro) leaves,
  roughly chopped
1 cup flat-leaf (Italian) parsley
  leaves, roughly chopped
1 teaspoon smoked paprika
1 teaspoon salt
125 ml (4 fl oz/½ cup) extra-virgin
  olive oil

Garlic & tahini yoghurt
125 g (4½ oz/½ cup) Greek-style
  yoghurt
juice of ½ lemon
1 tablespoon tahini
1 small garlic clove, crushed
¼ teaspoon ground cumin
sea salt flakes

To make the chermoula, toast the cumin and coriander in a small dry frying pan over medium heat for about 2 minutes until fragrant. Transfer to a food processor along with the remaining ingredients. Process until well combined.

Rub the chermoula all over the lamb shoulder, cover with plastic wrap and refrigerate for 2 hours or overnight.

Remove the lamb from the refrigerator 1 hour before cooking.

Preheat a hooded barbecue grill to medium–high and lightly grease with oil.

Cook the lamb skin-side down for 15 minutes. Turn and cook for a further 10 minutes. Reduce the heat to medium, cover and cook for a further 15 minutes. Remove from the heat, cover with foil and rest for 10 minutes.

To make yoghurt sauce, combine the ingredients in a small bowl.

Slice the lamb thinly, drizzle with the sauce and garnish with herbs to serve.

FEED THE MAN BEEF

Menu

BEEF

Is there anything better than a great big juicy steak grilling over hot flames? The smoky aromas, the hissing of juices and the sense of achievement when you nail that slightly charred crust and tender pink interior. There's just something a little bit primeval and a whole lot awesome about cooking slabs of meat over some fire.

While it's hard to resist diving into your perfectly cooked chunk of beef as soon as it comes off the heat, stay strong and let it rest for at least 5 minutes – the meat will stay juicier and tastier and you will be much, much happier.

When it comes to beef, there's no need to stop at steaks. Sixteen-year-olds in fast-food restaurants shouldn't get all the fun of flipping burgers on a grill; make your own big juicy beef patties for the ultimate boss burgers (page 90) or go Mexican with fresh and zesty beef fajitas (page 98).

BARBECUED STEAK
WITH BÉARNAISE SAUCE

→→ SERVES 4 ←←

4 porterhouse (strip) steaks
Chargrilled witlof (page 135),
   to serve (optional)

Béarnaise sauce
250 g (9 oz) butter
2 French shallots, finely chopped
2 tablespoons white-wine vinegar
2 large egg yolks
1 tablespoon lemon juice, plus
   extra if required
1 tablespoon finely chopped
   tarragon
1 tablespoon olive oil

To make the béarnaise sauce, heat 1 tablespoon of the butter in a small saucepan over medium heat. Add the shallots and a grind of black pepper and cook for 30 seconds. Add the vinegar, reduce the heat to medium–low, and cook for about 2–3 minutes until the vinegar has evaporated. Reduce the heat to low and continue cooking for about 5 minutes until the shallots are tender and translucent. Transfer to a small bowl to cool.

Heat the remaining butter in a small saucepan over medium heat for about 2–3 minutes until it foams. Transfer to a small jug and keep hot.

Combine the vinegar reduction with the egg yolks, lemon juice, tarragon and 1 tablespoon of water in a small food processor and blend until smooth. With the motor running, add the hot butter in a thin, steady stream, discarding the milk solids in the bottom of the jug. Continue blending for 2–3 minutes until a smooth, creamy sauce forms. Pour the sauce into a medium-sized bowl and season to taste with salt, pepper, and more lemon juice, if desired. Cover and keep warm. Béarnaise sauce can be served at room temperature, but it is very tricky to reheat if you let it go cold.

Brush the steaks with oil and season both sides lightly with salt and pepper. Cover and set aside for 20 minutes to bring to room temperature.

Preheat a barbecue grill to high and lightly grease with oil.

When the grill is smoking hot, cook the steaks for 4 minutes on each side for medium rare (you can cook a little less or more according to your preference). Remove from the heat, cover and rest for 5 minutes.

Serve with the béarnaise sauce and, if desired, Chargrilled witlof.

ARGENTINIAN BEEF RUMP
WITH CHIMICHURRI

→→ SERVES 6–8 ←←

2 kg (4 lb 6 oz) beef rump, with fat cap intact

Spice rub
1 tablespoon smoked sweet paprika
1 tablespoon sea salt flakes
2 teaspoons ancho chilli powder
1 teaspoon soft brown sugar
1 teaspoon ground black pepper

Chimichurri
2 cups flat-leaf (Italian) parsley leaves, roughly chopped
1 cup coriander (cilantro) leaves, roughly chopped
½ cup mint leaves, roughly chopped
3 garlic cloves, roughly chopped
2 French shallots, roughly chopped
2 long red chillies, deseeded and roughly chopped
60 ml (2 fl oz/¼ cup) lemon juice
2 tablespoons sherry vinegar or red-wine vinegar
1 teaspoon sea salt flakes
½ teaspoon freshly ground black pepper
185 ml (6 fl oz/¾ cup) extra-virgin olive oil

To make the spice rub, combine the ingredients in a small bowl.

Place the beef on a clean work surface and, using a sharp knife, score the fat in a crosshatch pattern. Cut deeply, but don't cut into the meat. (This will help to baste the meat as it cooks by evenly releasing the flavoursome fat, and it will also stop the sides of the meat from curling.) Massage the spice rub deeply into the grooves and all over the meat. Cover with plastic wrap and refrigerate for 2 hours.

To make the chimichurri, blend the parsley, coriander, mint, garlic, shallots, chilli, lemon juice, vinegar, salt and pepper in a food processor until a coarse paste forms. With the motor running, add the oil in a thin, steady stream until incorporated. Taste and adjust the seasoning, then transfer to a small bowl, cover with plastic wrap and refrigerate until needed.

Preheat a hooded barbecue grill to high and lightly grease with oil.

Place the beef, fat-side up, onto the grill, cover and reduce the heat to medium–low. Cook for 45 minutes. Turn the beef and cook for a further 15 minutes. Turn again and for another 10 minutes for medium. (You can cook a little less or more according to your preference). Transfer to a plate, cover loosely with foil and rest for 20 minutes before slicing.

Slice the beef thickly and serve on a platter drizzled with half the chimichurri. Serve the remainder of the sauce in a small bowl for guests to help themselves.

The Boss
BEEF BURGERS

500 g (1 lb 2 oz) minced (ground) lean beef
1 red onion, finely chopped
½ cup flat-leaf (Italian) parsley leaves, finely chopped
¼ cup basil leaves, finely chopped
¼ cup semi-sundried tomatoes, finely chopped
1 egg
½ teaspoon sea salt flakes
¼ teaspoon ground black pepper
¼ teaspoon sweet paprika
4 round bread rolls, split
4 slices gruyère cheese
iceberg lettuce leaves, to serve
2 gherkins (pickles), sliced
1 large tomato, sliced
ketchup, mustard, mayonnaise, relish and/or chilli sauce, to serve

Combine the beef, onion, parsley, basil, sundried tomato, egg, salt, pepper and paprika in a large bowl. Mix well by hand. Divide in four even portions and, with wet hands, press into flat patties slightly wider than the bread rolls. Transfer to a plate, cover with plastic wrap and rest in the fridge for 30 minutes. (The patties will keep in the refrigerator for a few hours, so they can be prepared ahead of time.)

Heat a barbecue hotplate (griddle) or grill to medium and lightly grease with oil.

Brush or spray the burgers lightly with olive oil. Cook, turning occasionally, for 10 minutes or until cooked through. When almost cooked, top each burger with a cheese slice to melt and then toast the buns lightly on both sides.

Spread the base of each bun with your sauce/s of choice then top with lettuce, gherkins, the burger and tomato slices. Spread the top with any other sauce, as desired, and dig in.

Veal Cutlets with
SAGE, CAPERS & LEMON

2 anchovies, roughly chopped
2 garlic cloves, finely chopped
1 tablespoon olive oil
4 x 250 g (9 oz) veal cutlets
2 lemons, halved
125 g (4½ oz) butter, coarsely
  chopped
1 tablespoon capers, drained
20 sage leaves
2 tablespoons lemon juice

In a small bowl, mash the anchovies with a fork. Stir in the garlic and olive oil. Brush the cutlets on both sides with the anchovy mixture, cover and set aside for 30 minutes.

Preheat a barbecue grill to high and lightly grease with oil.

Cook the cutlets for 5 minutes each side or until caramelised on the outside. Cook the lemon halves, cut-side down, for 3–4 minutes until beginning to char. Remove the veal and lemons from the heat, cover and rest for 5 minutes.

Reduce the heat to medium and place a small frying pan on the grill. Add the butter, and cook, swirling the pan to melt evenly, until the butter begins to foam. Add the capers and sage and cook until crisp. Mix in the lemon juice and remove from the heat.

Serve the cutlets topped with the sage, caper and lemon butter and with the charred lemon halves for squeezing.

RUMP STEAK WITH
CORIANDER & JALAPEÑO BUTTER

→→ SERVES 4 ←←

4 rump steaks, about 200 g (7 oz)
  each
Mexican corn on the cob
  (page 132), to serve (optional)
lime wedges, to serve
coriander (cilantro) leaves, to serve

**Coriander & jalapeño
butter**
80 g (2¾ oz/⅓ cup) butter,
  softened
2 small jalapeño chillies, deseeded
  and finely chopped
¼ cup coriander (cilantro) leaves,
  finely chopped
zest of ½ lime
½ teaspoon sea salt

To make the butter, combine the ingredients in a small bowl, mixing well with a fork. Lay a sheet of baking paper on a work surface and spoon the butter into a thick line in the centre. Roll into a log and chill until needed.

Preheat a barbecue grill to high and lightly grease with oil.

Brush the steaks with olive oil and season lightly with salt on both sides.

When the grill is smoking hot, cook the steaks for 4 minutes on each side for medium rare (you can cook a little less or more according to your preference). Remove from the heat, cover and rest for 5 minutes.

Slice the butter into discs and serve on top of the steaks. Great accompanied by Mexican corn on the cob.

Sticky Beef Short Ribs
WITH BOURBON-LACED
BARBECUE SAUCE

2 kg (4 lb 6 oz) beef short ribs, cut between bones into single ribs
Apple & cabbage slaw (page 134), to serve (optional)

Spice rub
1 tablespoon smoked paprika
2 teaspoons sea salt flakes
1 teaspoon freshly ground black pepper
3 garlic cloves, crushed
80 ml (2½ fl oz/⅓ cup) olive oil

Barbecue sauce
2 tablespoons olive oil
1 onion, finely chopped
2 garlic cloves, crushed
1 long red chilli, deseeded and finely chopped
80 ml (2½ fl oz/⅓ cup) cider vinegar
45 g (1½ oz/¼ cup softly packed) soft brown sugar
170 ml (5½ fl oz/⅔ cup) tomato passata (puréed tomatoes)
2 tablespoons lemon juice
80 ml (2½ fl oz/⅓ cup) pure maple syrup
2 teaspoons dijon mustard
2 tablespoons worcestershire sauce
80 ml (2½ fl oz/⅓ cup) bourbon

To make the spice rub, combine the ingredients in a small bowl. Coat the ribs with the rub, massaging the seasoning in well. Cover with plastic wrap and refrigerate for 2 hours.

Preheat the oven to 150°C (300°F).

Place the ribs in a baking tin in a single layer. Cook for 2–2½ hours until tender.

Meanwhile, to make the barbecue sauce, heat the oil in a medium-sized saucepan over medium–low heat. Cook the onion, stirring occasionally for 8–10 minutes until softened. Add the garlic and chilli and cook for a further 4 minutes. Add the vinegar, sugar, passata, lemon juice, maple syrup, mustard, worcestershire sauce and bourbon. Stir to combine and bring to the boil. Reduce heat and simmer for about 15 minutes or until it develops a thick pouring consistency. Season to taste and set aside to cool.

Preheat a barbecue grill to medium high and lightly grease with oil.

Brush the ribs with barbecue sauce and cook, turning regularly and basting, for 20–30 minutes until a charred and sticky crust forms. Serve with remaining barbecue sauce and, if desired, Apple & cabbage slaw.

Thai Chilli–Coconut
SURF & TURF SKEWERS

24 large raw prawns (shrimp),
  peeled, with tails left intact
300 g (10½ oz) rump or sirloin
  steak, thinly sliced across
  the grain
bamboo skewers, soaked in
  cold water
cucumber slices, to serve
mint leaves, to serve
lime wedges, to serve

Chilli–coconut marinade
300 ml (10 fl oz) coconut milk
2 lemongrass stalks, white part
  only, finely chopped
6 kaffir lime leaves, finely chopped
2 long red chillies, finely chopped
2 teaspoons grated palm sugar
zest and juice of 1 lime
2 tablespoons fish sauce
1 tablespoon kecap manis
2 tablespoons peanut oil

To make the marinade, combine the coconut milk, lemongrass, kaffir lime leaves and chilli in a small saucepan over low heat and simmer uncovered for 10 minutes. Set aside to cool to room temperature. Transfer to a food processor along with the palm sugar, lime zest and juice, fish sauce and kecap manis. Process until well blended. With the motor running, add the oil in a thin, steady stream until incorporated.

Divide the marinade between two large bowls, adding the beef and prawns to each separate bowl. Toss well to coat.

Thread the prawns and beef onto separate skewers, threading the prawns lengthways. Cover and refrigerate for 1 hour.

Preheat a barbecue grill to high and lightly grease with oil.

Cook skewers for 1–2 minutes each side or until just cooked through.

Serve with cucumber, mint leaves and lime wedges.

GRILLED BEEF FAJITAS
WITH SALSA & GUACAMOLE

→→ **SERVES 4–6** ←←

1 kg (2 lb 3 oz) beef skirt steak
2 red onions, halved and sliced
1 red capsicum (bell pepper), sliced
1 green capsicum (bell pepper), sliced
1 yellow capsicum (bell pepper), sliced
10 flour tortillas
150 g (5½ oz) queso fresco or feta cheese, crumbled
125 g (4½ oz/½ cup) sour cream

Marinade
125 ml (4 fl oz/½ cup) olive oil
3 garlic cloves, crushed
3 tablespoons soy sauce
juice of 2 limes
1 tablespoon soft brown sugar
1 tablespoon ground cumin
2 teaspoons ancho chilli powder
2 teaspoons chilli flakes
1 teaspoon sea salt flakes
½ teaspoon black pepper

Fresh tomato salsa
1 long red chili, finely chopped
250 g (9 oz) cherry tomatoes, roughly chopped
1 cup coriander (cilantro) leaves and stalks, roughly chopped
juice of 1 lime

Guacamole
1 avocado, peeled and diced
juice of ½ lime

To make the marinade, combine the ingredients in a small bowl and mix well.

Place the steaks in a dish and the onion and capsicum in a second dish. Divide the marinade between the dishes and mix to coat. Cover with plastic wrap and refrigerate for 2 hours.

To make the salsa, combine the ingredients in a small bowl. Season to taste. Cover and set aside until needed.

To make the guacamole, combine the ingredients in a bowl and mash roughly with a fork. Season to taste. Cover and set aside until needed.

Preheat a barbecue grill and hotplate (griddle) to high and lightly grease with oil.

Cook the steaks on the grill for 1–2 minutes, then turn. Cook for another 1–2 minutes, and turn again. Continue cooking, turning every minute or so, for 8–10 minutes in total, or until done to your liking. Transfer to a plate, cover loosely with foil and rest for 10 minutes.

Cook the capsicum and onion mix on the hotplate, turning occasionally, for about 5–8 minutes or until just cooked and slightly charred. Transfer to a serving platter and keep warm.

Cut the steaks diagonally into thin slices and transfer to the serving platter.

Briefly toast the tortillas on one side over the hot grill and stack onto a board. Serve with the salsa, guacamole, cheese and sour cream alongside.

FEED THE MAN
VEG

Menu

VEG

This might sound crazy, but grilling doesn't always have to be a meatfest. Whether you're feeding vegetarian mates or just want to get some more veg into your diet, grilling is a fantastic way to cook all kinds of vegetables as well as tofu and that king among cheeses, haloumi.

There are some vegetables that are just made for grilling: capsicum (bell pepper), asparagus, zucchini (courgette), onion, eggplant (aubergine) and corn are all born for the task – just a lick of olive oil and a touch of salt is all you need.

And your meat-avoiding friends will want to kiss you when you serve them up a big fat delicious edamame burger (page 118) or a mushroom quesadilla (page 108) – you may even be tempted to try them yourself.

Haloumi Burgers
WITH PEPERONATA

1 tablespoon olive oil
250 g (9 oz) haloumi, coarsely grated
150 g (5½ oz) sweet potato, coarsely grated
150 g (5½ oz) zucchini (courgettes), coarsely grated and squeezed to remove excess moisture
2 tablespoons finely chopped mint
2 tablespoons finely chopped flat-leaf (Italian) parsley
finely grated zest of 1 lemon
1 large egg
4 wholegrain burger buns, split
1 large handful baby spinach or lettuce leaves
1 large tomato, sliced

Peperonata
2 tablespoons olive oil
2 garlic cloves, finely sliced
½ teaspoon dried chilli flakes
1 small red onion, finely sliced
2 red capsicums (bell peppers), sliced into 1 cm (½ in) strips
¼ teaspoon sea salt flakes
½ teaspoon soft brown sugar

Heat the olive oil in a small frying pan over medium heat. Fry the sweet potato for 4–5 minutes until cooked and just beginning to caramelise. Set aside to cool.

In a large mixing bowl, combine the haloumi, sweet potato, zucchini, mint, parsley, lemon zest and egg.

Divide the mixture into four equal portions and, using wet hands, shape into patties. Cover with plastic wrap and refrigerate for at least 30 minutes to firm.

To make the peperonata, heat the olive oil in a medium-sized frying pan over medium heat. Add the garlic and chilli flakes, and cook gently for 1 minute. Add the onion and capsicum and cook, stirring frequently, for 15 minutes or until softened and beginning to caramelise. Add the salt and sugar and cook for a further 2 minutes.

Heat a barbecue hotplate (griddle) to medium and lightly grease with oil.

Brush or spray the burgers lightly with olive oil. Cook on the hotplate for 3–4 minutes on each side until golden brown, using a barbeque spatula to gently turn the burgers.

Toast the burger buns lightly on each side, then assemble each with baby spinach or lettuce, tomato, a burger patty and the peperonata.

Grilled Vegetable &
HALOUMI KEBABS

200 g (7 oz) haloumi, cut into
  2 cm (¾ in) cubes
2 yellow capsicums (bell peppers),
  cut into 2 cm (¾ in) chunks
2 medium zucchini (courgettes),
  sliced into 1 cm (½ in) rounds
200 g (7 oz) cherry tomatoes
2 red onions, cut into 2 cm (¾ in)
  chunks
bamboo skewers, soaked in cold
  water
salad leaves, to serve
lemon wedges, to serve
Yeasted grilled flatbreads
  (page 124), to serve (optional)

Marinade
60 ml (2 fl oz/¼ cup) olive oil
juice of 1 lemon
2 garlic cloves, crushed
1 red chilli, finely chopped
8 mint leaves, finely chopped
1 tablespoon dried oregano

To make the marinade combine the ingredients in a large bowl and whisk well. Add the haloumi, capsicum, zucchini, tomatoes and onion, and toss to coat.

Preheat a barbecue hotplate (griddle) to medium and lightly grease with oil.

Thread the haloumi and vegetables onto the skewers.

Cook the kebabs for 3–5 minutes on each side until the haloumi browns and the vegetables have slightly softened and caramelised.

Serve with salad leaves, lemon wedges and flatbread (if desired).

MIXED MUSHROOM
QUESADILLAS

2 tablespoons olive oil

2 French shallots, finely chopped

3 garlic cloves, finely chopped

400 g (14 oz) mixed mushrooms (such as portobello, brown, king, porcini, oyster, button, shimeji), sliced

2 jalapeño chillies, finely chopped

½ teaspoon sea salt flakes

¼ teaspoon freshly ground pepper

8 soft corn tortillas, taco size

1 cup grated cheese such as queso fresco, mozzarella, fontina, cotija or parmesan

⅓ cup coriander (cilantro) leaves, finely chopped, plus extra to garnish

Preheat a barbecue hotplate (griddle) to medium and lightly grease with oil.

In a large mixing bowl combine the olive oil, shallots, garlic, mushrooms, chillies, salt and pepper.

Cook on the hotplate, turning and stirring regularly, for 5–6 minutes, until the mushrooms and shallots become soft and begin to caramelise. Remove from the heat and set aside to cool slightly.

Top four tortillas with the mushroom mixture. Scatter the cheese and coriander over and top with a second tortilla. Place onto the hotplate and cook on both sides until golden brown and the cheese is melted.

Slice each quesadilla into quarters, garnish with coriander and serve immediately.

Note: Quesadillas can be made from 1 tortilla folded in half to make a half moon, or 2 tortillas filled to make a circle as described above. The half moon shapes are great for kids as the fold reduces spillage.

OKONOMIYAKI

150 g (5½ oz/1 cup) plain
  (all-purpose) flour
40 g (1½ oz/⅓ cup) cornflour
  (cornstarch)
¼ teaspoon salt
¼ teaspoon sugar
¼ teaspoon baking powder
185 ml (6 fl oz/¾ cup) vegetable
  stock
4 eggs
¼ cup pickled red ginger, plus
  extra to garnish
½ medium white or savoy
  cabbage, finely sliced
Okonomi sauce (see note),
  to serve
Japanese mayonnaise, to serve
8 spring onions (scallions), finely
  chopped

In a large bowl, combine the flour, cornflour, salt, sugar and baking powder. Add the stock, whisk well and refrigerate the batter for 1 hour.

Preheat a hooded barbecue hotplate (griddle) to medium and lightly grease with oil.

Add the eggs and pickled ginger to the batter and mix well. Stir in the cabbage.

Pour ladles of batter onto the oiled hotplate to make eight pancakes. Cover and cook for 5 minutes until browned on the bottom. (The cover helps the thick pancake cook through to the centre.) Turn, cover and cook for 5 minutes until browned. Turn once more and cook, uncovered, for another 2 minutes.

To serve, drizzle with Okonomi sauce and Japanese mayo and garnish with spring onion and pickled ginger.

Note: Okonomi sauce is available from Asian grocery stores. A quick substitute sauce can be made by blending 3 tablespoons tomato ketchup, 1 tablespoon vegetarian worcestershire sauce, 1 tablespoon mushroom soy sauce and 2 teaspoons of sugar.

Southern-style
BARBECUED TOFU

2 blocks (600 g/1 lb 5 oz total)
  extra-firm tofu, cut into quarters
  then drained and dried
Apple & cabbage slaw (page 134),
  to serve (optional)

Dry rub
1 teaspoon ground coriander
1 teaspoon ground cumin
2 teaspoons dried oregano
2 teaspoons sweet paprika
1 teaspoon smoked paprika
1 teaspoon garlic powder
1 teaspoon soft brown sugar
1 teaspoon ground cinnamon
2 teaspoons sea salt
1 teaspoon freshly ground
  black pepper

Preheat a barbecue grill to high heat and lightly grease with oil.

To make the rub, combine all of the ingredients in a small bowl.

Coat the tofu on all sides with the rub.

Cook for about 4 minutes or until golden brown. Turn and cook for a further 4 minutes.

Remove from the heat and, if you like, serve with a side of Apple & cabbage slaw.

Hommus & Za'atar

GRILLED VEGETABLE WRAPS

→ SERVES 4 ←

2 red capsicums (bell peppers), cut into 5 cm (2 in) pieces
2 zucchini (courgettes), sliced lengthways into 1 cm (½ in) strips
2 eggplants (aubergines), sliced into 1 cm (½ in) rounds
1 red onion, sliced into rings
4 large flatbread wraps
Roast chickpea and garlic hommus (page 139), to serve
100 g (3½ oz) baby spinach leaves
¼ cup mint leaves

Za'atar marinade
1 tablespoon dried thyme
1 tablespoon sesame seeds
2 teaspoons sumac
½ teaspoon salt
60 ml (2 fl oz/¼ cup) olive oil
juice of ½ lemon

Preheat a barbecue hotplate (griddle) and grill to medium and lightly grease with oil.

To make the za'atar marinade, combine the ingredients in a large bowl and whisk well.

Brush the capsicum, zucchini and eggplant with the marinade then place on the grill. Cook, turning once, for 4–6 minutes. Toss the onion in the remaining marinade and cook on the hotplate for 8–10 minutes until tender and beginning to caramelise.

Toast the wraps on the grlll briefly to soften.

Assemble the wraps by spreading each with a heaped tablespoon of hommus, and topping with a handful of spinach leaves, and the capsicum, zucchini, eggplant, onion and mint leaves before rolling up to serve.

Korean
BULGOGI TOFU

600 g (1 lb 5 oz) firm tofu, drained
  and cut into cubes
½ onion, finely sliced
4 spring onions (scallions), finely
  sliced
12 iceberg lettuce leaves
2 cucumbers, cut into short spears
2 tablespoons sesame seeds,
  toasted

Marinade
185 ml (6 fl oz/¾ cup) tamari
½ onion, finely chopped
½ nashi pear, cored and grated
2 garlic cloves, crushed
1 teaspoon grated ginger
2 tablespoons soft brown sugar
1 teaspoon chilli flakes
½ teaspoon freshly ground black
  pepper
1 tablespoon sesame oil

To make the marinade, combine the ingredients in a small bowl.

Pour a little bit of marinade into the base of a dish, add the tofu, and pour the remaining marinade over. Cover and refrigerate for 20 minutes.

Preheat a barbecue hotplate (griddle) to medium and lightly grease with oil.

Cook the onion, spring onions and tofu, turning the tofu after 4–5 minutes and continue cooking until caramelised.

Serve the tofu cubes in lettuce leaves with cucumber spears and sprinkled with sesame seeds.

Barbecued
MEDITERRANEAN PIZZA
WITH BASIL OIL & RICOTTA

2 zucchini (courgettes), cut
  diagonally into 1 cm (½ in) slices
1 yellow capsicum (bell pepper),
  cut into strips
1 red capsicum (bell pepper), cut
  into strips
½ red onion, sliced into wedges
5 field mushrooms, sliced
200 g (7 oz) ricotta cheese
50 g (1¾ oz) grated parmesan
  cheese

Pizza dough
185 ml (6 fl oz/¾ cup) warm water
½ teaspoon active dried yeast
350 g (12½ oz/2 ⅓ cups) strong
  flour
½ teaspoon sea salt flakes
3 tablespoons olive oil, plus extra
  for coating

Basil oil
60 ml (2 fl oz/¼ cup) extra-virgin
  olive oil
½ cup basil leaves
2 garlic cloves, thinly sliced

To make the pizza dough, place the water in a small bowl and sprinkle the yeast over. Set aside for a few minutes until frothy. Combine the flour and salt in the bowl of an electric mixer fitted with a paddle attachment. Turn on to low speed and drizzle in the olive oil until combined. Slowly pour in the yeast mixture and mix until a sticky dough forms. Form the dough into a ball, cover with a little olive oil and place in a lightly oiled mixing bowl. Cover with plastic wrap and set aside in a warm place for 1–2 hours until the dough has doubled in size.

To make the basil oil, heat the oil in a small saucepan over medium–low heat. Add the basil leaves and garlic and swirl the pan until the leaves are wilted and the oil has become fragrant and turned a rich green colour.

Preheat a hooded barbecue grill to high and lightly grease with oil.

Brush the zucchini, capsicums, onion and mushrooms with half the basil oil. Grill, turning occasionally, until the vegetables are tender and have defined grill marks. Set aside.

In a small mixing bowl, mash the ricotta and parmesan together with a fork.

Lightly grease a 28 cm x 40 cm (11 in x 16 in) rectangular baking tray or two round pizza trays. On a floured surface, roll out the pizza dough to fit the tray or trays. Brush the remaining basil oil over the base, adding the basil leaves and garlic. Scatter spoonfuls of the cheese over the base, and arrange the zucchini, capsicums, onion and mushroom over the top.

Place the tray or trays over the barbecue grill and close the lid. Cook for about 10–15 minutes until the crust is golden brown.

EDAMAME BURGERS
WITH RED ONION JAM

6 full-sized or 10 mini sourdough
  rolls
lettuce leaves, to serve
3 tomatoes, sliced
2 Lebanese cucumbers, sliced
  diagonally

Red onion jam
60 ml (2 fl oz/¼ cup) olive oil
500 g (1 lb 2 oz) red onions, thinly
  sliced
2 sprigs thyme
1 bay leaf
1 long red chilli, thinly sliced
2 tablespoons soft brown sugar
1 teaspoon sea salt flakes
¼ teaspoon freshly ground black
  pepper
2 tablespoons balsamic vinegar

Edamame patties
80 g (2¾ oz/½ cup) cashews
80 g (2¾ oz/½ cup) grated carrot
1 small onion, diced
2 garlic cloves, roughly chopped
½ cup flat-leaf (Italian) parsley
  leaves, chopped
1 tablespoon tamari
120 g (4½ oz/2 cups) podded
  edamame beans
110 g (4 oz/1 cup) besan
  (chickpea flour)

To make the red onion jam, heat the oil in a medium-sized saucepan over medium heat. Add the onion, thyme, bay leaf and chilli. Cook, stirring regularly, for 25–30 minutes or until softened and golden. Add the sugar, salt, pepper, vinegar and 125 ml (4 fl oz/½ cup) of water. Bring to the boil then reduce the heat to low. Simmer, uncovered, for 8–10 minutes or until thick and jammy.

To make the patties, blend the cashews, carrot, onion, garlic, parsley, tamari and half the edamame in a food processor until it forms a chunky paste. Transfer to a large bowl. Add remaining the beans and the besan, season to taste and mix well. Cover with plastic wrap and refrigerate for 30 minutes (this will make it easier to handle when forming the patties).

Preheat a barbecue hotplate (griddle) to medium and lightly grease with oil.

Form the edamame mix into 6 or 10 patties and cook for 4–5 minutes each side or until golden.

Place the lettuce and patties on the rolls and top with tomato, cucumber and red onion jam.

FEED THE MAN
SIDES & SALADS

Menu

SIDES & SALADS

Sure, you may not be able to make friends with salad, but what's a big juicy steak all on its own? Some bitter leaves or a grilled cabbage salad (page 150) turns a slab of meat into a sophisticated meal.

If you've never cooked baked jacket potatoes on your grill then it's time to start. You can go for simple, classic topping combos like cheese and coleslaw, or really bring the class with smoked trout and horseradish crème (pages 142–143).

And when you've gone to the trouble of making your own sausages, then you can't let the team down with shop-bought ketchup. Make the tomato ketchup recipe on page 149 for the full homemade experience.

Yeasted Grilled FLATBREAD

→→ **MAKES 4** ←←

300 g (10½ oz/2 cups) strong flour
1 teaspoon sea salt flakes
1½ teaspoons active dried yeast
3 teaspoons butter, softened
about 150 ml (5 fl oz) warm water

Place the flour, salt and yeast in a large mixing bowl. Add the butter and two-thirds of the water and mix by hand until the mixture comes together. Mix in enough of the remaining water for a dough to form.

Tip onto a lightly floured surface and knead the dough for 7–8 minutes until smooth and silky. Return the dough to the mixing bowl, cover with a clean damp dish towel and set aside in a warm place for about 1 hour, until the dough has doubled in size.

Preheat a barbecue hotplate (griddle) to medium high and lightly grease with oil.

Flour your surface again. Tip the dough onto the surface and knock back to get the air out. Divide the dough into six portions and roll into balls. Roll out into ovals about ½ cm (¼ in) thick. Transfer to a lightly-oiled baking tray and set aside for 10–15 minutes.

Place the flatbreads on the hotplate and cook for about 3–4 minutes on each side until browned and blistered.

Serve immediately.

Unleavened Grilled
FLATBREAD

→→ **MAKES 4** ←←

300 g (10½ oz/2 cups) strong
   flour, plus extra if needed
¼ teaspoon ground cumin
¼ teaspoon ground coriander
¾ teaspoon sea salt flakes
50 g (1¾ oz) butter, melted
185 ml (6 fl oz/¾ cups) warm milk

In a large bowl, combine the flour, cumin, coriander, salt, butter and milk until a dough forms.

Tip onto a lightly floured surface and knead the dough for a few minutes until smooth. If the dough is too sticky, add a little extra flour. Wrap with plastic wrap and rest at room temperature for 30 minutes.

Preheat a barbecue hotplate (griddle) to medium high and lightly grease with oil.

Flour your surface again. Divide the dough into four portions and roll into balls. Roll out into rounds about ½ cm (¼ in) thick.

Place the flatbreads on the hotplate and cook for about 1 minute on each side, turning when the dough begins to bubble.

Serve immediately.

Yeasted grilled flatbread (left);
Unleavened grilled flatbread (right).

Summer Veg

RATATOUILLE PARCELS

→ **SERVES 4–6 AS A SIDE** ←

2 red onions, halved and thickly sliced
4 garlic cloves, unpeeled
1 eggplant (aubergine), sliced into 1 cm (½ in) rounds
2 zucchini (courgettes), cut lengthways into 1 cm (½ in) strips
2 red capsicums (bell peppers), halved and cut into strips
80 ml (2½ fl oz/⅓ cup) extra-virgin olive oil
½ teaspoon sea salt flakes
½ teaspoon freshly ground black pepper
4 thyme sprigs, leaves removed
500 g (1 lb 2 oz) tomatoes, deseeded and diced
2 teaspoons balsamic vinegar
basil leaves, to garnish

Preheat a barbecue hotplate (griddle) and grill to medium and lightly grease with oil.

In two separate bowls, toss the onion and garlic, and the eggplant, zucchini and capsicum in the olive oil.

Cook the onion and garlic on the hotplate, and the eggplant, zucchini and capsicum on the grill. Cook for 6–8 minutes, turning occasionally, until softened and caramelised.

Transfer to a mixing bowl along with the salt, pepper, thyme, tomatoes and balsamic vinegar. Toss to combine well.

Tear four 1 metre (1 yard) sheets of foil, and fold in half to make a double layer. Cut sheets of baking paper slightly smaller than the foil to place on top.

Use a slotted spoon to divide the vegetables evenly between the four sheets, placing the vegetables into the centre of each. Lift the sides up and seal along the side edges by folding over twice (about 2 cm (¾ in) for each fold), leaving the tops open.

Divide the remaining juices from the bowl between the parcels, then fold the tops to seal, folding twice as before, but ensuring you leave some room for steam.

Reduce the barbecue heat to low and cook the parcels on the grill for 20 minutes.

Vegetable parcels can be served hot or at room temperature, garnished with basil leaves. Be careful when opening the foil parcels as the steam inside will be very hot.

Barbecued
POTATO WEDGES
WITH LIME YOGHURT

→→ **SERVES 4 AS A SIDE** ←←

4 large floury potatoes, cut into
   wedges about 3 cm (1¼ in) thick
80 ml (2½ fl oz/⅓ cup) olive oil

Seasoning
1 teaspoon sweet paprika
1 teaspoon of ancho chilli powder
1 teaspoon sea salt flakes
½ teaspoon soft brown sugar

Lime yoghurt
185 g (6½ oz/¾ cup) Greek-style
   yoghurt
zest of ½ lime
2 teaspoons chopped coriander
   (cilantro) leaves

Preheat a barbecue grill to medium high and lightly grease with oil.

To make the seasoning, combine the paprika, chilli, salt and sugar in a small bowl.

Bring a large saucepan of salted water to the boil over high heat. Boil the potato wedges for 5 minutes. Drain well.

To make the lime yoghurt, mix the yoghurt, lime zest and coriander in a small bowl.

Brush the wedges with olive oil and place on the grill. Cook for 5–6 minutes on each side or until browned and crispy on the outside and tender inside.

Transfer the potatoes to a large bowl. Sprinkle with the spice mixture and toss to coat. Serve immediately with lime yoghurt alongside for dipping.

HERBY NEW POTATO
SALAD

500 g (1 lb 2 oz) small red new potatoes
½ teaspoon dijon mustard
½ teaspoon sea salt flakes
¼ teaspoon freshly ground black pepper
60 ml (2 fl oz/¼ cup) olive oil
1 small red onion, very finely diced
2 tablespoons chopped chives
1 tablespoon chopped flat-leaf (Italian) parsley

Place the potatoes in a medium-sized saucepan over high heat and cover with cold water. Bring to the boil, then reduce heat to medium–low and simmer for 10–15 minutes until tender when tested with a skewer (be careful not to overcook as the skins may split and the potatoes will become waterlogged). Drain and set aside to cool slightly.

In a small bowl, combine the mustard, salt, pepper and olive oil.

Cut the potatoes into bite-sized pieces and place in a medium-sized bowl along with the onion. Pour the dressing over while the potatoes are still hot, and toss to combine.

Allow to cool.

Stir the chives and parsley through before serving.

Mexican Corn
ON THE COB

→→ **SERVES 4 AS A SIDE** ←←

4 corn cobs, husks removed
smoked paprika, for sprinkling
¼ cup finely grated manchego or
    parmesan cheese
1 lime, quartered, to serve

Chipotle mayo
juice of 1 lime
1 tablespoon chipotle sauce
125 g (4½ oz/½ cup) good-quality
    whole egg mayonnaise

Heat a barbecue grill to high and lightly grease with oil.

Blanch the corn in a large saucepan of boiling water for 1 minute, then drain.

To make the chipotle mayo, combine the ingredients in a small bowl, stirring to combine well.

Brush or spray the corn with olive oil and cook on the grill, turning occasionally, for about 10 minutes or until charred. Transfer to a serving platter.

Spread a small spoonful of chipotle mayo over each cob. Sprinkle with smoked paprika and cheese.

Serve with any remaining chipotle mayonnaise and with lime wedges for squeezing.

Apple & Cabbage
SLAW

¼ small red cabbage, finely shredded

¼ small green cabbage, finely shredded

2 small granny smith apples, cut into matchsticks

4 spring onions (scallions), finely sliced

1 cup coriander (cilantro) leaves, roughly chopped

Dressing

2 tablespoons lime juice

1 tablespoon cider vinegar

2 teaspoons dijon mustard

½ teaspoon salt

2 tablespoons olive oil

Combine the cabbage, apple, spring onions and coriander in a large salad bowl.

To make the dressing, combine the lime juice, vinegar, mustard, salt and olive oil in a small bowl.

Pour the dressing over the salad and toss to combine well.

CHARGRILLED WITLOF

4 large witlof (chicory/Belgian
endive), halved lengthways
olive oil, for drizzling
juice of 1 lemon
1 tablespoon finely chopped
flat-leaf (Italian) parsley

Preheat a barbecue grill to high and lightly grease with oil.

Brush the witlof halves with oil and season lightly with salt and freshly ground black pepper.

Place the cut-side down for 2–3 minutes, then turn and cook on the other side for another 2 minutes.

To serve, drizzle with a little extra olive oil and the lemon juice, and sprinkle with parsley.

PORTUGUESE SALAD

3 green capsicums (bell peppers)
6 roma (plum) tomatoes
3 garlic cloves, unpeeled
pinch of sea salt flakes
pinch of dried chilli flakes
60 ml (2 fl oz/¼ cup) extra-virgin
  olive oil
2 tablespoons sherry vinegar
1 baby cos (romaine) lettuce,
  leaves separated
½ cup coriander (cilantro) leaves

Preheat a barbecue grill to high and lightly grease with oil.

Place the capsicums, tomatoes and garlic cloves on the grill to cook, turning occasionally with tongs, until the skins are charred and blistered all over. Transfer to a bowl, cover with plastic wrap and set aside to cool.

Peel the skins from the capsicums, tomatoes and garlic. Remove and discard the capsicum seeds and chop tomatoes and capsicums roughly.

Pound the garlic, salt and chilli flakes into a paste using a mortar and pestle. Combine with the olive oil and sherry vinegar to make a dressing.

Combine the capsicum, tomato, lettuce and coriander in a salad bowl. Pour the dressing over and toss to combine.

Grilled Eggplant
WITH SAGE OIL

12 sage leaves, finely chopped,
  plus extra to garnish
1 teaspoon sea salt flakes
100 ml (3½ fl oz) olive oil
2 eggplants (aubergines), sliced
  lengthways

Combine the sage leaves, salt and olive oil in a small bowl. Brush the slices of eggplant with the sage oil. Allow to stand for 1 hour.

Preheat a barbecue grill to medium and lightly grease with oil.

Grill the eggplant slices for 2–3 minutes on each side until soft, and grill marks appear. Garnish with sage leaves to serve.

Note: Look for eggplants that have glossy skins and fresh green stems.

ROASTED CHICKPEA
& GARLIC HOMMUS

200 g (7 oz) dry chickpeas
4 garlic cloves, unpeeled
2 tablespoons olive oil
1 teaspoon sea salt flakes
2 tablespoons lemon juice
½ teaspoon ground cumin
135 g (5 oz/½ cup) tahini
za'atar (see page 113, but make without the olive oil and lemon juice), to garnish
extra-virgin olive oil, for drizzling

Soak the chickpeas overnight in 1 litre (34 fl oz/4 cups) cold water. Rinse and drain well. Transfer the chickpeas to a large saucepan and cover with 1.5 litres (51 fl oz/6 cups) water. Simmer gently, covered, for about 1½ hours or until very tender. Drain, reserving the cooking liquid. Rinse the chickpeas in water and drain again.

Preheat the oven to 180°C (350°F).

In a medium-sized bowl, combine the chickpeas, garlic cloves and olive oil. Spread onto a baking tray lined with baking paper and bake for 20 minutes or until the chickpeas start to colour. Remove from the oven and set aside to cool a little.

When cool enough to handle, squeeze the garlic from the skins. Place the garlic and chickpeas in a food processor along with the salt, lemon juice, cumin, tahini and 170 ml (5½ fl oz/⅔ cup) of the reserved chickpea cooking liquid.

Pulse for a few minutes, or until creamy. Adjust the thickness if required by adding a little warm water. The hommus will thicken on standing. Transfer to a small serving bowl and sprinkle with za'atar and drizzle with extra-virgin olive oil.

Grilled Cauliflower & Sweet
POTATO SALAD
WITH TAHINI–YOGHURT DRESSING

→→ SERVES 4 AS A SIDE ←←

1 cauliflower, cut into florets

500 g (1 lb 2 oz) sweet potato, peeled, cut into 2 cm (¾ in) pieces

1 large red onion, cut into thin wedges

2 garlic cloves, crushed

2 cm (¾ in) piece ginger, grated

1 long red chilli, finely chopped

80 ml (2½ fl oz/⅓ cup) extra-virgin olive oil

400 g (14 oz) tinned chickpeas, rinsed and drained

⅔ cup coriander (cilantro) leaves, chopped

Spice mix

2 teaspoons ground cumin

2 teaspoons ground coriander

1 teaspoon ground cinnamon

½ teaspoon ground allspice

Tahini–yoghurt dressing

125 g (4½ oz/½ cup) Greek-style yoghurt

1 tablespoon tahini

1 clove garlic, crushed

1 tablespoon lemon juice

Preheat a barbecue hotplate (griddle) to medium and lightly grease with oil.

To make the spice mix, combine the ingredients in a small bowl.

In a large bowl, combine the cauliflower, sweet potato, onion, garlic, ginger, chilli and olive oil.

Cook the vegetable mix on the hotplate, turning regularly, for 8–10 minutes or until the sweet potato is cooked through. Return to the mixing bowl and set aside to cool.

To make the dressing, combine the ingredients in a bowl.

Add the chickpeas to the vegetables and then sprinkle the spice mix and coriander over the top. Stir through to combine well.

Pour the dressing over the salad just before serving and toss well to coat.

Barbecued
BAKED POTATOES

→→ **SERVES 4** ←←

4 whole washed potatoes or small sweet potatoes

Preheat a hooded barbecue grill to medium and grease with oil.

Poke a few deep holes in the potatoes with a metal skewer. Wrap each potato in two layers of foil, ensuring they are well covered.

Place the potatoes on the grill and cover. Cook for 30 minutes, then turn and cook for another 20–30 minutes longer, until the flesh is tender (test by inserting a metal skewer).

Remove the foil from the potato and cook, turning occasionally, for 10 minutes, until browned all over.

Serve with any of the toppings opposite.

AVOCADO, FETA & DUKKAH

1 tablespoon almonds
1 tablespoon pistachio nuts
1 tablespoon pine nuts
2 teaspoons coriander seeds
2 teaspoons cumin seeds
1 tablespoon sesame seeds
½ teaspoon sea salt flakes
pinch of cinnamon
pinch of nutmeg
Barbecued baked potatoes
  (see recipe left)
100 g (3½ oz) feta cheese,
  crumbled
1 avocado, mashed roughly

Toast the almonds and
pistachios in a large frying
pan over medium-high heat,
stirring, for 5 minutes until just
starting to colour and become
fragrant. Set aside and add the
pine nuts and coriander seeds
to the hot pan. Toast and stir
for a minute, and then add
the cumin and sesame seeds.
Continue to toast, stirring,
until golden brown.

Using a mortar and pestle,
pound the nuts, toasted
spices, salt, cinnamon and
nutmeg until coarsely ground.

Split the tops of the baked
potatoes and fill with feta
and avocado and sprinkle
with dukkah.

SMOKED TROUT & HORSERADISH CRÈME

200 g (7 oz) crème fraiche
2 teaspoons finely grated horseradish
2 tablespoons chopped chives
200 g (7 oz) smoked trout, flaked
  into small chunks
Barbecued baked sweet potatoes
  (see recipe left)
¼ red onion, finely chopped
lemon wedges to serve

In a medium-sized bowl,
combine the crème fraiche,
horseradish and chives.
Gently stir in the smoked trout.

Split the tops of the sweet
potatoes and fill with smoked
trout mixture. Add a teaspoon
of red onion to the top of each
and serve with lemon wedges
for squeezing.

CHEESE & SPRING ONION COLESLAW

75 g (2¾ oz/1 cup) finely sliced red
  cabbage
75 g (2¾ oz/1 cup) finely sliced
  green cabbage
1 carrot, grated
1 tablespoon white vinegar
1 teaspoon caster (superfine) sugar
1 teaspoon sea salt flakes
3 tablespoons whole egg
  mayonnaise
4 spring onions (scallions), finely
  chopped
120 g (4½ oz) aged cheddar
  cheese, grated

In a medium-sized mixing
bowl, combine the cabbage
and carrot. Sprinkle with the
vinegar, sugar and salt and
toss to combine well. Set aside
for 1 hour.

The cabbage will release
liquid, so drain and squeeze
out any excess moisture. Place
the drained cabbage mixture
into a clean mixing bowl
along with the mayonnaise
and spring onions and stir
to combine.

Split the tops of the potatoes
and fill with cheddar cheese.
Place the potatoes back on
the grill, close the hood and
cook for 4–5 minutes until the
cheese has melted. Top with
coleslaw to serve.

Clockwise from top left: Cheese & spring onion coleslaw;
Avocado, feta & dukkah; Smoked trout & horseradish crème.

Mexican
QUINOA SALAD

2 corn cobs, husks removed
300 g (10½ oz/1½ cups) red
   quinoa, rinsed thoroughly
250 g (9 oz) grape tomatoes,
   halved
1 red capsicum (bell pepper), diced
1 red onion, finely diced
1 jalapeño chilli, very finely diced
400 g (14 oz) tinned black beans,
   rinsed and drained
2 cups coriander (cilantro) leaves,
   finely chopped
30 g (1 oz/¼ cup) pepitas
   (pumpkin seeds)

Dressing
2 tablespoons olive oil
juice of 2 limes
½ teaspoon sea salt flakes
1 teaspoon smoked paprika
½ teaspoon ground cumin

Heat a barbecue grill to high and lightly grease with oil.

Blanch the corn in a large pot of boiling water for 1 minute, then drain. Brush or spray the corn with olive oil and cook on the grill, turning occasionally, for about 10 minutes or until charred. Set aside to cool then cut the kernels off the cobs.

Bring 750 ml (25½ fl oz/3 cups) of water to boil in a medium saucepan over high heat. Add the quinoa, cover and simmer for about 15 minutes or until all the moisture is absorbed. Remove from the heat and keep covered.

To make the dressing, combine the ingredients in a small bowl and whisk well.

To assemble the salad, mix the quinoa, corn, tomatoes, capsicum, onion, chilli and beans in a large bowl. Pour the dressing over, add the coriander and toss to combine. Sprinkle with the pepitas.

Serve at room temperature.

TURKISH

ROASTED TOMATO SALAD

→→ **SERVES 4–6 AS A SIDE** ←←

6 medium roma tomatoes
4 large long red sweet peppers
  (such as bullhorn or cubanelle)
2 red capsicums (bell peppers),
  finely chopped
1 bunch flat-leaf (Italian) parsley,
  leaves finely chopped
1 red onion, coarsely chopped

Dressing
2 garlic cloves, finely chopped
½ teaspoon chilli flakes
1 teaspoon sweet paprika
1 teaspoon sea salt flakes
1 tablespoon lemon juice
60 ml (2 fl oz/¼ cup) extra-virgin
  olive oil
1 tablespoon pomegranate
  molasses

Preheat a barbecue grill to medium–high and lightly grease with oil.

Cook the tomatoes and sweet peppers over the grill, turning occasionally, for 6–8 minutes until the skins are blackened and blistering. Seal in a plastic container or bag and set aside to cool. Remove and discard the skins, stems and seeds. (Don't rinse as it will wash away the delicious charred flavour.)

Finely chop the tomato and pepper flesh and transfer to a large mixing bowl. Add the capsicum, parsley and onion and mix to combine.

To make the dressing, combine the ingredients in a small bowl. Stir well to blend.

Pour the dressing over the salad and toss well. Cover and refrigerate for 1 hour to allow the flavours to develop.

Serve at room temperature.

Homemade
TOMATO KETCHUP

3 kg (6 lb 10 oz) tomatoes, roughly chopped
2 granny smith apples, cored and roughly chopped
1 onion, roughly chopped
1 cinnamon stick
2 garlic cloves, crushed
1 teaspoon freshly ground black pepper
1 teaspoon ground allspice
600 g (1 lb 5 oz) raw caster (superfine) sugar
2 tablespoons sea salt flakes
400 ml (13 ½ fl oz) cider vinegar

Place all the ingredients in a large saucepan over low heat. Simmer for 2 hours, uncovered, stirring frequently or until the sauce reduces and thickens to a saucy consistency.

Strain the mixture through a fine-meshed sieve into a large bowl, pressing down to extract the liquid. Discard solids.

Pour the hot mixture into sterilised bottles and seal. Store in a cool, dark place until ready to use. Once opened, the sauce will keep for up to 1 month in the refrigerator.

GRILLED
CABBAGE SALAD

45 g (1½ oz/¼ cup) palm sugar
60 ml (2 fl oz/¼ cup) lime juice
2 tablespoons fish sauce
2 garlic cloves, crushed
½ green cabbage, cut into thin
  wedges
¼ red cabbage, cut into thin
  wedges
2 tablespoons peanut oil
2 red Asian shallots, finely diced
1 long red chili, thinly sliced

Preheat a barbecue hotplate (griddle) to medium and lightly grease with oil.

Combine the palm sugar, lime juice, fish sauce and garlic in a small saucepan over low heat. Simmer for 3–4 minutes until the sugar has dissolved and the mixture has reduced by a third. Remove from the heat.

Brush the cabbage wedges with the peanut oil and cook on the hotplate for 6–8 minutes on each side, allowing the edges to blacken slightly.

Transfer to a chopping board and remove the cores from the cabbage. Place the cabbage wedges in a serving bowl and pour the dressing over.

Garnish with the shallots and chilli.

FEED THE MAN
DESSERT

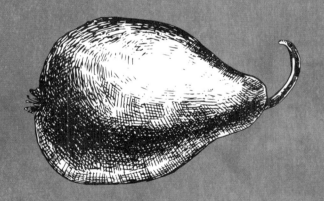

Menu

DESSERT

A man should always have a few surprises up his sleeve. There are certain things a guest expects at a barbecue: sausages, steaks, salads – no surprises there. But imagine the look of awe and amazement on your friends' faces as they watch you whipping up a deluxe hot dessert using the very grill you used to cook their chops. They'll be talking about it for years. Really. (Probably.)

Fruits with firm flesh, particularly stone fruits, do really well on the grill. Just slice in half and place the cut side on the heat and grill until the sugars caramelise and you're on your way to sweet, sticky, smoky goodness. Top that with a slug of something boozy like rum or bourbon and you've got yourself a seriously potent dessert.

Grilled Pineapple with
CINNAMON SUGAR & MINT

1 pineapple, peeled, cored and cut
  lengthways into 8 wedges
8 bamboo skewers, soaked in cold
  water
1 tablespoon softened butter
140 g (5 oz/¾ cup) soft brown
  sugar
2 teaspoons ground cinnamon
pinch of sea salt flakes
mint leaves, to serve

Thread the pineapple wedges onto the skewers.

Preheat a barbecue grill to medium and lightly grease with oil.

In a small saucepan, cook the butter and brown sugar over low heat, stirring until melted. Add the cinnamon and salt and mix well. Remove from the heat.

Brush the sugar syrup over the pineapple wedges and cook on the grill for 3–5 minutes on each side, until caramelised.

Serve hot on a platter scattered with mint leaves.

CHERRY & CHOCOLATE
DESSERT PIZZA

➤➤ **SERVES 6** ◂◂

½ teaspoon active dried yeast
1 tablespoon caster (superfine)
  sugar
1 tablespoon softened butter
80 ml (2½ fl oz/⅓ cup) warm milk
125 ml (4 fl oz/½ cup) warm water
300 g (10½ oz/2 cups) strong flour
½ teaspoon sea salt flakes
50 g (1¾ oz) mascarpone cheese
2 teaspoons soft brown sugar
zest of ½ lemon
2 cups cherries, pitted
shaved dark chocolate, for topping
mint leaves, to garnish

In a large jug, combine the yeast, caster sugar, butter, milk and water and stir well. Set aside for a few minutes.

Place the flour and salt in a large mixing bowl and make a well in the centre. Pour the yeast mixture into the well and, using a spatula, draw the flour over the liquid to incorporate, until a dough forms. Tip onto a lightly floured work surface and knead the dough for 8 minutes until smooth.

Return the dough to the bowl and cover with a clean damp dish towel. Leave to rise in a warm place for 1 hour or until the dough has doubled in size.

Preheat a hooded barbecue grill to medium–high and lightly grease with oil.

Knead the dough again lightly to knock out the air. Roll out into a circle, about 25 cm (10 in) in diameter, and place on a lightly oiled pizza tray.

In a small bowl, combine the mascarpone, brown sugar and lemon zest, then spread the mixture over the dough base. Arrange the cherries evenly over the top, lightly pressing into the dough.

Place the tray onto the grill, cover and cook for 15–20 minutes until the base is well cooked.

Remove from the heat and scatter with chocolate and mint leaves. Slice and serve.

Grilled Peaches
WITH MASCARPONE
& CARAMEL SAUCE

→→ **SERVES 4** ←←

35 g (1¼ oz/¼ cup) whole
  hazelnuts
4 peaches, halved and stones
  removed
1 tablespoon softened butter
75 g (2¾ oz/⅓ cup) mascarpone
  cheese

Caramel sauce
140 g (5 oz/¾ cup) soft brown
  sugar
185 ml (6 fl oz/¾ cup) cream
zest of ½ lemon

Preheat barbecue grill to medium low and lightly grease with oil.

Heat a small frying pan over medium heat and toast the hazelnuts
for 1–2 minutes until toasted and fragrant. Set aside to cool and
then roughly chop.

To make the caramel sauce, combine the sugar with 60 ml
(2 fl oz/¼ cup) of water in a small saucepan over low heat, stirring
until the sugar has melted. Use a wet pastry brush to brush down
the side of the pan to dissolve any remaining sugar crystals. Bring
to the boil and cook, stirring, for about 8 minutes until the mixture
turns a light golden colour. Remove from the heat immediately.
Set aside to cool for a few minutes then stir in the cream and
lemon zest. The mixture may foam a little. Stir until smooth.

Brush the cut sides of the peaches generously with butter and
place, cut-side down, onto the grill. Cook for 4–5 minutes or
until grill marks appear.

Remove from the heat and serve immediately topped with
mascarpone, caramel sauce and hazelnuts.

Barbecued Pears with
CINNAMON & HONEY
CRÈME FRAÎCHE

>> SERVES 4 <<

4 firm beurre bosc or packham
    pears, cored, unpeeled
4 cinnamon sticks
125 ml (4 fl oz/½ cup) honey
½ teaspoon ground cinnamon
100 g (3½ oz) crème fraîche, to
    serve
thyme leaves, to garnish

Preheat a hooded barbecue grill to medium–low and lightly grease with oil.

Place a cinnamon stick in the hollowed core of each pear.

Wrap the pears in a double layer of foil and place on the grill. Cover and cook for 30 minutes.

Combine the honey and cinnamon with 125 ml (4 fl oz/½ cup) of water in a small saucepan over low heat. Cook, stirring occasionally, for 5 minutes or until the syrup thickens slightly. Set aside to cool.

Unwrap the cooked pears and serve whole. Add a dollop of crème fraîche and spoon the cinnamon and honey syrup over the top. Garnish with thyme leaves.

Grilled Figs
WITH ROSEMARY
& POMEGRANATE RICOTTA

→ SERVES 4 ←

200 g (7 oz) ricotta cheese
1 tablespoon pomegranate
  molasses, plus extra to serve
1 tablespoon lemon juice
1 tablespoon soft brown sugar
1 tablespoon finely chopped
  rosemary, plus extra sprigs
  to garnish
8 fresh figs, halved lengthways
25 g (1 oz/¼ cup) walnut halves

Preheat a barbecue grill to medium and lightly grease with oil.

Heat a small frying pan over medium heat and toast the walnuts for 1–2 minutes until fragrant. Set aside to cool, then roughly chop.

Whisk the ricotta and pomegranate molasses together in a medium-sized mixing bowl.

In a small bowl, combine the lemon juice, sugar and rosemary. Stir to dissolve the sugar.

Brush the cut side of the figs with the lemon mixture, then place, cut-side down, onto the grill. Cook for 3–4 minutes or until grill lines appear and the figs are hot through.

Arrange the figs on serving plates with the ricotta and walnuts. Garnish with rosemary sprigs, and drizzle with a little extra pomegranate molasses.

NECTARINES
WITH CITRUS & KAFFIR LIME SYRUP

4 ripe nectarines, halved and
  stones removed
1 tablespoon melted coconut oil
vanilla bean or coconut ice cream,
  to serve (optional)
mint leaves, to garnish

Citrus & kaffir lime syrup
230 g (8 oz/1 cup) caster
  (superfine) sugar
80 ml (2½ fl oz/⅓ cup) lime juice
60 ml (2 fl oz/¼ cup) orange juice
1 tablespoon lemon juice
3 kaffir lime leaves, shredded
¼ cup mint leaves

To make the syrup, combine the sugar and the lime, orange and lemon juice with 80 ml (2½ fl oz/⅓ cup) water in a medium-sized saucepan over medium heat. Simmer until thickened and slightly syrupy. Add the kaffir lime and mint leaves and remove from the heat. Set aside for 20 minutes for the flavours to infuse.

Preheat a barbecue grill to medium–high and lightly grease with oil.

Brush the nectarine halves with coconut oil and grill for 3–5 minutes on each side until grill marks appear.

Strain the leaves from syrup. If the syrup has become too thick (it needs to pour), reheat gently and stir in a tablespoon of water.

Serve the nectarines with a scoop of ice cream (if you like) and a drizzle of the syrup. Garnish with mint leaves.

Rum-Spiked Barbecued
BANANA BOATS

4 bananas
60 g (2 oz/⅓ cup) dark chocolate chips
20 g (¾ oz/¼ cup) shredded coconut, toasted
1 teaspoon ground cinnamon
2 tablespoons honey
2 tablespoons dark rum
vanilla bean ice cream, to serve (optional)

Preheat a hooded barbecue grill to medium and lightly grease with oil.

Using four pieces of heavy duty foil, shape a support for each banana by scrunching the foil up around the sides of the bananas, so they won't tip over while cooking on the grill.

Combine the chocolate, coconut, cinnamon, honey and rum in a small mixing bowl. Cut a slit into the bananas lengthways, leaving 2 cm (¾ in) intact at each end. Cut deeply, but not through the skin at the back. Divide the chocolate mixture between the bananas.

Place the bananas in their foil boats on the grill. Cover and cook for 4–5 minutes or until the skins have blackened and the chocolate has melted.

If you like, serve the bananas with a scoop of ice cream.

FEED THE MAN
NOW!

INDEX

Mexican corn on the cob 132

Mexican quinoa salad 146

Mint & garlic lamb kebabs with
    quinoa tabouli 78

Mixed mushroom quesadillas 108

Moroccan lamb meatballs with
    minted yoghurt 70

N, O

Nectarines with citrus & kaffir lime
    syrup 164

Okonomiyaki 110

P

peaches with mascarpone &
    caramel sauce, Barbecued 160

pears with cinnamon & honey
    crème fraîche, Barbecued 162

peri peri chicken, Barbecued 16

pineapple with cinnamon sugar &
    mint, Grilled 156

pizza with basil oil & ricotta ,
    Barbecued Mediterranean 116

pizza, Cherry & chocolate dessert
    158

po'boy, Louisiana prawn 54

Pork tenderloin with maple,
    ginger & orange glaze 38

Pork

Grilled pork ribs with
    Vietnamese dipping sauce 40

Homemade pork & fennel
    sausages 42

Jamaican jerk pork belly 43

Korean barbecued pork 46

Pork tenderloin with maple,
    ginger & orange glaze 38

Southern-style baby back pork
    ribs 44

Portuguese salad 136

potato salad, Herby new 131

potato wedges with lime yoghurt,
    Barbecued 130

potatoes, Barbecued baked 142

Q

quesadillas, Mixed mushroom 108

quinoa salad, Mexican 146

quinoa tabouli, Mint & garlic lamb
    kebabs with 78

R

Rack of lamb with rosemary
    crust 77

ratatouille parcels, Summer
    veg 128

ribs with bourbon-laced barbecue
    sauce, Sticky beef short 94

ribs with Vietnamese dipping
    sauce, Grilled pork 40

ribs, Southern-style baby back
    pork 44

Roasted chickpea & garlic
    hommus 139

Rum-spiked barbecued banana
    boats 166

Rump steak with coriander &
    jalapeño butter 93

S

Salads

Apple & cabbage slaw 134

Grilled cabbage salad 150

Grilled cauliflower & sweet
    potato salad 140

Herby new potato salad 131

Mexican quinoa salad 146

Portuguese salad 136

Turkish roasted tomato salad
    148

salmon with fennel & celery
    remoulade, Crispy skin 64

satay chicken skewers, Spicy 30

sausages, Homemade pork &
    fennel 42

Seafood

Japanese calamari 60

Lobster tail & salad sliders 62

Louisiana prawn po'boy 54

Thai chilli–coconut surf & turf
    skewers 96

Sides

Barbecued baked potatoes 142

Barbecued potato wedges
    with lime yoghurt 130

Chargrilled witlof 135

Grilled eggplant with sage oil
    138

Mexican corn on the cob 132

Summer veg ratatouille
    parcels 128

skewers, Brazilian cachaça
    chicken 18

skewers, Spicy satay chicken 30

snapper with Thai flavours,
    Whole 58

Smith Street Books

Published in 2016 by Smith Street Books
Melbourne | Australia
smithstreetbooks.com

ISBN: 978-1-925418-10-1

CIP data is available from the National Library of Australia

Publisher: Paul McNally
Senior Editor & introductory text: Hannah Koelmeyer, Tusk studio
Recipe development: Sue Herold
Design concept: Kate Barraclough
Design layout: Heather Menzies, Studio31 Graphics
Photographer & Stylist: Billy Law

Printed & bound in China by C&C Offset Printing Co., Ltd.
Book 9
10 9 8 7 6 5 4 3 2 1